The Hajj

SYED ABUL HASAN ALI NADWI

Translated By
Mohammad Asif Kidwai

NADWI PRESS

NADWI PRESS

Nadwi Press Edition

Find our titles on your favourite online bookstore using the keyword 'Nadwi Press'

Originally Published by AIRP, Lucknow (India)
Reprinted by Nadwi Press in 2025

Translation of the Qur'ān

It should be perfectly clear that the Qur'ān is only authentic in its original language, Arabic. Since perfect translation of the Qur'ān is impossible, we have used the translation of the meaning of the Qur'ān throughout the book, as the result is only a crude meaning of the Arabic text.

Qur'ānic verses appear in speech marks proceeded by a reference to the Surah and verse number. Sayings (Hadith) of Prophet Muhammad (saw) appear in inverted commas along with reference to the Hadith Book and its Reporter.

Foreword

In the name of Allah, the beneficent, the merciful

One of my books entitled, *the four pillars-in the light of the book and the sunnah and with a comparative study of modes of worship in other religions* has recently been published by Darul Fath (Beirut), and its Urdu and English editions have also been brought out by the academy of Islamic research and publications, Lucknow. In it light has been shed on the four fundamental duties in Islam- *Salat* (regular prayer), *Zakat* (poor-due), *Roza* (fasting), and *haj* (pilgrimage), and their aims and mysteries have been explained as proved by the Quran and the confirmed practice of the holy prophet and accepted through the ages by the Muslim legists and theologians.

My endeavour has been to bring out the true spirit and significance of the primary modes of worship by lifting the veil the unislamic customs and practices, exotic beliefs and ideas, and the curious interpretations of the faith that are politically motivated or influenced by the western thought have cast over them. I have also compared the various forms of Islamic worship with the religious laws, rituals and traditions of the other faiths, particularly Judaism, Christianity and Brahminism. It is a matter of gratification to me that the book has been warmly received in the theological and literary circles all over the world.

Some friends have suggested that the part of it dealing with haj should be published separately for this Act of worship is deserving of special heedfulness and Attention. The remoteness of mecca from the Islamic World and the fact that the pilgrimage is enjoined to be Performed by a Muslim once in his lifetime have contributed to its uniqueness. People come from the four Corners of the world to carry it out, they undergo all sorts of hardships, and travel by air, land and sea. It is, Therefore, essential that they understood its aims and Mysteries properly and appreciated its true inner significance. Besides, no other religious duty has been subjected more to modern ways of thinking and political attitudes and interests, so much so that many educated persons, even Muslim thinkers and writers, do not consider the haj pilgrimage to be more than an international Islamic conference which is held every year and possesses only a political or collective utility.

I agreed with the suggestion of the friends because in these pages, haj has been presented within its true Islamic framework and its profound meaning and far-reaching objects, and the real Ibrahimi and Hanafi spirit have been brought into view.

The booklet is meant primarily for the hajis and the pilgrims to the house of Allah, and for those who know only the English language so that they may realise the fundamental nature, significance and purpose of the pilgrimage before undertaking it and partake of its joys in the fullest measure and carry out its rites and formalities with a thorough understanding of them.

Daira Shah Alam ullah

Rae Bareli   Abul Hasan Ali Nadwi

August 25, 1974

The Hajj (pilgrimage)

﴿وَأَذِّن فِي ٱلنَّاسِ بِٱلۡحَجِّ يَأۡتُوكَ رِجَالٗا وَعَلَىٰ كُلِّ ضَامِرٖ يَأۡتِينَ
مِن كُلِّ فَجٍّ عَمِيقٖ ٢٧ لِّيَشۡهَدُواْ مَنَٰفِعَ لَهُمۡ وَيَذۡكُرُواْ ٱسۡمَ
ٱللَّهِ فِيٓ أَيَّامٖ مَّعۡلُومَٰتٍ عَلَىٰ مَا رَزَقَهُم مِّنۢ بَهِيمَةِ ٱلۡأَنۡعَٰمِۖ
فَكُلُواْ مِنۡهَا وَأَطۡعِمُواْ ٱلۡبَآئِسَ ٱلۡفَقِيرَ ٢٨ ثُمَّ لۡيَقۡضُواْ تَفَثَهُمۡ
وَلۡيُوفُواْ نُذُورَهُمۡ وَلۡيَطَّوَّفُواْ بِٱلۡبَيۡتِ ٱلۡعَتِيقِ ٢٩﴾

Call ⌜all⌝ people to the pilgrimage. They will come to you on foot and on every lean camel from every distant path, so they may obtain the benefits ⌜in store⌝ for them and pronounce the Name of Allah on appointed days over the sacrificial animals He has provided for them. So, eat from their meat and feed the desperately poor. Then let them groom themselves, fulfil their vows, and circle the Ancient House.” (22: 27-29)

Islam is a religion of pure monotheism. It does not admit of any intermediaries or intercessors between man and his creator.[1] It frowns upon all material and visible objects which might become centres of devotion and to which people paid spiritual homage in one form or another. There is no place in it for an intervening agency, a manifestation, an image or an idol. There is also no priestly class in Islam nor a tribe of monks and hermits.

﴿وَإِذَا سَأَلَكَ عِبَادِى عَنِّى فَإِنِّى قَرِيبٌۖ أُجِيبُ دَعْوَةَ ٱلدَّاعِ
إِذَا دَعَانِۖ فَلْيَسْتَجِيبُوا۟ لِى وَلْيُؤْمِنُوا۟ بِى لَعَلَّهُمْ يَرْشُدُونَ ١٨٦﴾

When My servants ask you ⌜O Prophet⌝ about Me: I am truly near. I respond to one's prayer when they call upon Me. So let them respond ⌜with obedience⌝ to Me and believe in Me, perhaps they will be guided ⌜to the Right Way⌝. (2: 186)

---

[1] Excepting, of course, the apostles in the sense that in the preaching and propagation of the divine call and in expounding the divine attributes and lending guidance along the straight path, they form an essential link between god and his bondmen, and faith itself is dependent upon the duty they discharge as revealers and interpreters of the divine will.

﴿إِنَّآ أَنزَلْنَآ إِلَيْكَ ٱلْكِتَٰبَ بِٱلْحَقِّ فَٱعْبُدِ ٱللَّهَ مُخْلِصًا لَّهُ
ٱلدِّينَ ٢ أَلَا لِلَّهِ ٱلدِّينُ ٱلْخَالِصُ ۚ وَٱلَّذِينَ ٱتَّخَذُوا۟ مِن دُونِهِۦٓ
أَوْلِيَآءَ مَا نَعْبُدُهُمْ إِلَّا لِيُقَرِّبُونَآ إِلَى ٱللَّهِ زُلْفَىٰٓ إِنَّ ٱللَّهَ
يَحْكُمُ بَيْنَهُمْ فِى مَا هُمْ فِيهِ يَخْتَلِفُونَ ۗ إِنَّ ٱللَّهَ لَا يَهْدِى مَنْ
هُوَ كَٰذِبٌ كَفَّارٌ ٣﴾

Indeed, we have sent down the Book to you ⌜O Prophet⌝ in truth, so worship Allah ⌜alone⌝, being sincerely devoted to Him. Indeed, sincere devotion is due ⌜only⌝ to Allah. As for those who take other lords besides Him, ⌜saying⌝, "We worship them only so they may bring us closer to Allah. (-39: 2-3)

Islam dwells at such a high level of intellectual purity, high-mindedness, honesty of purpose and sincerity of action that it is impossible to conceive of a better ideal or a nobler concept. No other faith or philosophy in the world can compare with it in these respects, nor can anyone improve upon the description given in the Quran of the uniqueness and excellence of the lord.

﴿لَيۡسَ كَمِثۡلِهِۦ شَيۡءٞۖ وَهُوَ ٱلسَّمِيعُ ٱلۡبَصِيرُ ١١﴾

There is nothing like Him, for He ⌜alone⌝ is the All-Hearing, All-Seeing. (42: 11)

Landmarks of Allah

But human nature being what it is, the quest for something within the perceptible phenomena through which one could seek the satisfaction of the inward impulse of love, adoration and submission has always formed a part of his essential character and personality.

For the fulfilment of this need, God has appointed certain visible and material objects which are consecrated to him and bear a special relation to his blessed name and are held popularly to be his own and upon which there is so much of his grace that the mere sight of them evokes his remembrance. Besides, with them are associated events, rites and experiences that serve as the portents of Allah, and remind us of his faith and the fortitude and endeavour of his apostles. He has been pleased to give to these objects the name of the landmarks of Allah, and to proclaim that to pay reverence to them is to pay reverence to him while to show disrespect to them is to show disrespect to him. He has permitted, or, rather, invited mankind to gratify its innate urge for love, closeness and observation through them.

﴿ذَٰلِكَۖ وَمَن يُعَظِّمۡ شَعَٰٓئِرَ ٱللَّهِ فَإِنَّهَا مِن تَقۡوَى ٱلۡقُلُوبِ ٣٢﴾

That is so. And whoever honours the symbols of Allah, it is certainly out of the piety of the heart. (-22: 32)

﴿ذَٰلِكَۖ وَمَن يُعَظِّمۡ حُرُمَٰتِ ٱللَّهِ فَهُوَ خَيۡرٞ لَّهُۥ عِندَ رَبِّهِۦۗ﴾

That is so. And whoever honours the rituals of Allah, it is best for them in the sight of their Lord. (22: 30)

Instinct of love

Man is neither wholly a rational animal nor is he so helpless as to be obliged to make his submission to any law or authority. He is also not a part in a machine which moves along a set course and according to a fixed law. He is mind as well as heart, faith as well as intuition and submission as well as love. It is in the many-sidedness of his personality that lies the secret of his greatness and nobility, and it is through it that he has been able to overcome seemingly insuperable obstacles and perform superhuman deeds. What is more, it was on account of this grand peculiarity of his being that he was entrusted with the 'responsibility' the heavens, the earth and the mountains he declined to shoulder and has succeeded in rising to heights that are the envy of the angels.

The bond between man and his creator is not only of a legal or logical character that may be limited to the payment of dues, the observance of laws and the enjoyment of rights. It is also a bond of love and other sublime emotions like those of devotion, tenderness and self-effacement and its scope is so wide that no human thought and deed has remained unaffected by it. Islam does not forbid this love. On the other hand, it calls us to it, encourages it and sustains it.

Says the Quran:

﴿وَٱلَّذِينَ ءَامَنُوٓاْ أَشَدُّ حُبًّا لِّلَّهِ﴾

But the ⌜true⌝ believers love Allah even more. (2: 165)

﴿قُلۡ إِن كَانَ ءَابَآؤُكُمۡ وَأَبۡنَآؤُكُمۡ وَإِخۡوَٰنُكُمۡ وَأَزۡوَٰجُكُمۡ وَعَشِيرَتُكُمۡ وَأَمۡوَٰلٌ ٱقۡتَرَفۡتُمُوهَا وَتِجَٰرَةٞ تَخۡشَوۡنَ كَسَادَهَا وَمَسَٰكِنُ تَرۡضَوۡنَهَآ أَحَبَّ إِلَيۡكُم مِّنَ ٱللَّهِ وَرَسُولِهِۦ وَجِهَادٖ فِي سَبِيلِهِۦ فَتَرَبَّصُواْ حَتَّىٰ يَأۡتِيَ ٱللَّهُ بِأَمۡرِهِۦۗ وَٱللَّهُ لَا يَهۡدِي ٱلۡقَوۡمَ ٱلۡفَٰسِقِينَ ٢٤﴾

Say, ⌜O Prophet⌝, "If your parents and children and siblings and spouses and extended family and the wealth you have acquired and the trade you fear will decline and the homes you cherish—⌜if all these⌝ are more beloved to you than Allah and His Messenger and struggling in His Way, then wait until Allah brings about His Will. Allah does not guide the rebellious people." (9: 24)

The Quran, while speaking of the divine apostles, draws pointed attention to their qualities of love, earnestness and self-sacrifice. Of prophet Yahya (john), for instance, it says:

﴿يَٰيَحۡيَىٰ خُذِ ٱلۡكِتَٰبَ بِقُوَّةٖۖ وَءَاتَيۡنَٰهُ ٱلۡحُكۡمَ صَبِيّٗا ١٢
وَحَنَانٗا مِّن لَّدُنَّا وَزَكَوٰةٗۖ وَكَانَ تَقِيّٗا ١٣﴾

⌜It was later said⌝, "O John! Hold firmly to the Scriptures." And We granted him wisdom while ⌜he was still⌝ a child, as well as purity and compassion from Us. And he was God-fearing. (19: 12-13)

The wonderful episode of Hazrat Ibrahim (Abraham) is a saga of love and dedication. The Quran specifically mentions how Hazrat Ibrahim placed the knife on the throat of his son and did not remove it till god had witnessed the depth and intensity of his sincerity, fortitude and sacrifice.

﴿وَنَٰدَيۡنَٰهُ أَن يَٰٓإِبۡرَٰهِيمُ ١٠٤ قَدۡ صَدَّقۡتَ ٱلرُّءۡيَآۚ إِنَّا كَذَٰلِكَ
نَجۡزِي ٱلۡمُحۡسِنِينَ ١٠٥ إِنَّ هَٰذَا لَهُوَ ٱلۡبَلَٰٓؤُاْ ٱلۡمُبِينُ ١٠٦﴾

We called out to him, "O Abraham! You have already fulfilled the vision." Indeed, this is how We reward the good-doers. That was truly a revealing test. (37: 104-6)

﴿إِنَّ إِبۡرَٰهِيمَ لَحَلِيمٌ أَوَّٰهٞ مُّنِيبٞ ٧٥﴾

Truly, Abraham was forbearing, tender-hearted, and ever turning ⌜to his Lord⌝. (11: 75)

Love is generated by the knowledge of the attributes if the Quran has dwelt at length on the attributes, functions and bounties of the lord it is mainly because the knowledge of the divine attributes holds the key to the sentiments of love and devotion. Scholars like Imam Ibn-i-Taimiyah have defined the Qur'anic method of explaining the essential and permanent qualities of the almighty creator as 'conciseness of the negative' And 'diffuseness of the positive'. It is the detailed description of the benevolent attributes of God and their signs and portents that feeds the flame of love within the human breast and fills it up with fervour and enthusiasm. If the negative attributes are the mentors of the mind, the positive attributes are the mentors of the heart.[2] without the knowledge of the beautiful names of

---

[2] In the Quran where the negative attributes of god are set forth, i.e., where it is explained what god is not, only short phrases like naught is his likeness have been used while where his positive attributes

god and his immaculate qualities, with which the holy Quran and the traditions are replete and which have been a constant source of joy and inspiration to his devoted servants, faith would have got reduced to a dogma and lost its capacity to stir the innermost recesses of the heart and to move it to its depths with sincerity and humbleness during prayer and repentance.

Without it, the relationship between God and man would have been a mechanical, qualified and restrained relationship in which there was neither breadth nor flexibility nor enthusiasm, and life, a dull, dry and narrow affair, bereft of the sweet madness of love and the delightfully poignant bite of desire.

Were this celestial wealth to be taken away from man what would be left to distinguish between life and death, between humanity and the vegetable kingdom?

Worthless is the cup that never overflows to quench the thirst of the spirit and to calm down the flame of love it was needed that the heart and the eyes

---

are mentioned, i.e., it is expounded what he is, the discussion is both detailed and forceful as in the last section of *Sura-i-hashr*.

of a Muslim should overflow from time to time, and, thus, provide an outlet for the agonizing feelings of loneliness and separation that are rising within the depths of his being of what use is the cup that gets filled to the brink but never overflows?

The Haj

Imam Ghazali was alive to the fact that love was the genuine need of a sensitive human being which he was always seeking to satisfy. The house of Ka'aba (at mecca), and all the landmarks of Allah that are associated with it, and the haj, with the rites and formalities which go to make it, contain an ideal provision for the gratification of this basic human urge and necessity.

﴿وَإِذۡ بَوَّأۡنَا لِإِبۡرَٰهِيمَ مَكَانَ ٱلۡبَيۡتِ أَن لَّا تُشۡرِكۡ بِي شَيۡـٔٗا
وَطَهِّرۡ بَيۡتِيَ لِلطَّآئِفِينَ وَٱلۡقَآئِمِينَ وَٱلرُّكَّعِ ٱلسُّجُودِ ٢٦ وَأَذِّن
فِي ٱلنَّاسِ بِٱلۡحَجِّ يَأۡتُوكَ رِجَالٗا وَعَلَىٰ كُلِّ ضَامِرٖ يَأۡتِينَ مِن كُلِّ
فَجٍّ عَمِيقٖ ٢٧ لِّيَشۡهَدُواْ مَنَٰفِعَ لَهُمۡ وَيَذۡكُرُواْ ٱسۡمَ ٱللَّهِ فِيٓ
أَيَّامٖ مَّعۡلُومَٰتٍ عَلَىٰ مَا رَزَقَهُم مِّنۢ بَهِيمَةِ ٱلۡأَنۡعَٰمِۖ فَكُلُواْ مِنۡهَا

وَأَطْعِمُوا۟ ٱلْبَآئِسَ ٱلْفَقِيرَ ﴿٢٨﴾ ثُمَّ لْيَقْضُوا۟ تَفَثَهُمْ وَلْيُوفُوا۟
نُذُورَهُمْ وَلْيَطَّوَّفُوا۟ بِٱلْبَيْتِ ٱلْعَتِيقِ ﴿٢٩﴾

And ⌜remember⌝ when We assigned to Abraham the site of the House, ⌜saying⌝, "Do not associate anything with Me ⌜in worship⌝ and purify My House for those who circle ⌜the Ka'bah⌝, stand ⌜in prayer⌝, and bow and prostrate themselves. Call ⌜all⌝ people to the pilgrimage. They will come to you on foot and on every lean camel from every distant path, so they may obtain the benefits ⌜in store⌝ for them and pronounce the Name of Allah on appointed days over the sacrificial animals He has provided for them. So, eat from their meat and feed the desperately poor. Then let them groom themselves, fulfil their vows, and circle the Ancient House." (22: 26-29)

Imam Ghazali writes, "if there is an earnest desire for nearness to god, a Muslim will be compelled to strive for it. A lover is passionately attached to everything that bears an association with the beloved. The house of ka 'aba is associated with god, and a Muslims should, therefore, instinctively feel drawn to it, to speak nothing of the attraction of the recompense promised on it."[3]

Writing in the same vein, Hazrat Shah Waliullah remarks, "Sometimes, when a man is overcome with the desire for his lord and love surges powerfully in his breast, and he looks around for the satisfaction of his inner urge, it appears to him that the haj alone is the means to it."[4]

The salat a man offers up several times a day could be regarded as sufficient to fulfil the need of soothing and gratifying his emotions. It could have provided him with an opportunity to give vent to his feelings and to alleviate the agony of separation by shedding a few tears during it. But these tears could not quench his thirst. They could only suppress it for the time being for they did not possess the power to put down the all-consuming fire of love which, sometimes, turned the heart into a blazing furnace.

---

[3] *Ihya-ul-uloom*, vol. I, p. 24.

[4] *Hujjatullah-il-Baligha*, vol. I, p. 59.

Golden cage of materialism

Likewise, fasting could be helpful in slaking the thirst of the soul and curbing the intensity of animal appetites for hunger and abstinence do possess a purificatory quality. But the hours of fasting are limited, and they are also often surrounded by things that do not go well with it. An atmosphere of slothfulness and gormandising gets created around the person who fasts, and the society in which he lives has itself become so permissive of sensuality and godlessness that he feels isolated like an island in a sea.

A Muslim, therefore, had to be furnished with an opportunity to take a bold and adventurous plunge which could break his chains and release him from the old and dingy prison-house of everyday existence. It was to be in the nature of a leap which could, in one stride, carry him from this rotten, hide-bound, calculating and artificial life to a new, fascinating and boundless world where love reigned supreme, and the heart held sway over everything, where he was delivered from every kind of servitude and deification, and the man-made limitations of race, geography and politics died away and melted into nothingness, and where the creed of pure and unalloyed monotheism of the unity of godhead, providence, humanity, faith and purpose-became the bedrock of his way of living and he, along with his brethren, sang enthusiastically the praises of the lord and raised the heart-warming cry of:

O god, here I am! Here I am in thy presence! Thou art without a partner! Here I am! All praise is for thee and from thee are all blessings! To thee alone belongs power and rule! Thou art without a partner.

Even after the prayer-service a Muslim celebrates regularly every day, the fasting he observes yearly in the month of Ramadhan and the poor-due he pays, provided that he possesses the taxable minimum of wealth, at the end of each year there was the need for him of a special period of time, of a season of enchantment and adoration, eccentricity and infatuation.

Revolt against the worship of matter

It was also necessary for a Muslim to rebel, once in a while, against the cold and cheerless intellect. A life which is not occasionally shaken by tumult and revolt is not worth living. A man should, at times, liberate himself by breaking the fictitious bonds of habit and custom, of pedantic law, artificial taboos and stereotyped conventions, and handing over the control of his affairs to the heart. He should, at least once in a lifetime, go into wilderness in the manner of a dejected lover and give a proof of the sweet madness of love as the wont is of the people of faith and sensitiveness for only then can he have a taste of real freedom. Who will call him free who is permanently a slave to convention and society? How can a person be a true monotheist when he is a prisoner of his own habits, desires and inclinations? How can he be considered loyal and faithful if he is always obeying the dictates of the mind, and unless he weighs everything in the scales of his created intellect and its material advantages become apparent to him, he cannot arouse himself to a deed of devotion and fidelity?

The haj, in its particular form, is entirely opposed to the self-imposed laws and the mechanical routine of life the worshippers of matter and intellect and the prisoners of discipline and orderly conduct are addicted to. What it aims at is that faith in the unseen and the urge and ability to carry out an order, blindly and unhesitatingly- simply because it is an order-may take root in one's inner self, and the cold and calculating intellect may be dispossessed, for a time, of its authority which weighs and balances everything and lays stress only on its logical and perceptible aspect.

Imam Ghazali has delved deep into the spirit and purpose of the haj and drawn an excellent portrait of it with his inimitable pen. He says:

"In its nature and design the house of Allah is like a regal court to which adorers and admirers and those stricken with the torment of separation come from far and near, way-worn, haggard and dishevelled, with their heads bowed in submission and the conviction of their wretchedness embedded in their hearts forgetting themselves before his glory and magnificence and knowing fully well and affirming wholeheartedly that he is too sublime, too exalted to be encompassed by a boundary- wall or contained in a city or town, so that their devotion and servitude and crying and lamentation may reach its limit and nothing is left wanting by way of obeisance and self-surrender.

"That is why they are required to carry out certain acts and perform certain rites that lie beyond the domain of the intellect, such as, *rami jemar*[5] and *sa'ee*[6]. All these acts signify the highest form of slavery and bondage. Zakat is an exercise in compassion the purpose of which is easily understood. Saum is a spiritual discipline for self-purification and suppression of the evil propensities the devil exploits in order to gain his end, and in it the aspect of devoting oneself to prayer by cutting down other engagements is manifest. In *Salat* the greatness and glory of the lord and the bondman's own humbleness is revealed through *Ruku*, sujud and other acts which are also conducive to meekness and self-abasement. Bul *rami jemar* and *sa'ee* and the other rituals of the haj impart no joy or satisfaction to the heart. They do not appeal to human nature and the intellect also does not discover any sense or purpose in them. These acts are performed solely in a spirit of obedience, knowing that it is the command of God which has to be carried out in any event. The idea is to divest

---

[5] The throwing of pebbles at Satan.

[6] The ritual of covering, at a brisk pace, seven times each way, the distance between the two points of Safa and Marwa.

the mind of its authority and dominance and to keep the self away from things for which it may develop an inclination because when the mind fully accepts a thing the heart automatically gets inclined to it and the inner bent or liking itself becomes the mainspring of action. The spirit of complete surrender and submission is, thus, lost in its observance. It was said by the prophet pointedly at the time of the haj, 'here I am for the haj with a true heart and in a spirit of obeisance and servility.' the prophet did not use these words for any other mode of worship including salat.

"Since god, in his wisdom, has made salvation dependent upon the carrying out of duties with loyalty, devotion and humbleness, the devotional acts and observances (whose inner significance is beyond the understanding of man) are more efficacious in diverting the attention from self-purification and virtuousness to complete self-surrender."[7]

Of the ritual of *rami jemar*, Imam Ghazali tells that its very essence lies in absolute submission to a divine command. "its aim", writes he, "is abstract obedience

---

[7] *Ihya-ul-uloom*, vol. I., p. 240.

and compliance with commands, irrespective of their nature, so that complete servitude became evident. Reason or volition have nothing to do with it. It, further, signifies a resemblance with Hazrat Ibrahim for it was at this place that the accused devil had tried to tempt him and to create a doubt in his mind about the haj pilgrimage and Hazrat Ibrahim was inspired by God to throw pebbles at him so that he left him alone. Now, if someone were to imagine that Hazrat Ibrahim had thrown pebbles at the devil because he had appeared before him in reality but since, in his own case the devil was not to be seen, it was senseless to carry out the formality, he should know that this notion, too, had been planted in his mind by the devil in order to weaken his resolve to humble him."

"know that," he goes on to stress, "apparently you throw the pebbles at *jemaratul 'uqubah* (the last pillar) but, in fact, they hit the devil in the face and break his back for nothing humiliates him more than the carrying out of a divine command solely out of reverence for him and in a spirit of loyalty and obedience, without choice or intellect having a share in it."[8]

Similarly, about Qurbani (sacrificial offering of animals), Imam Ghazali observes:

"Know that compliance with the command of Qurbani is a means to the propitiation of Allah. It should be carried out readily and, in the hope, and expectation that God, in his mercy, will protect each and every limb of yours from the fire in return for each and every limb of the animal sacrificed by you. That is how it occurs in the traditions. The bigger the sacrificed animal is, the greater will the reward be on it."[9]

Absolute obedience

What the haj signifies is nothing more and nothing less than blind faith and total submission. It stands for unqualified obedience and earnest yielding to a demand. Sometimes, the pilgrim is seen in Mecca, and, sometimes, in *mina*, *arafat* and *muzdalifa*. Sometimes, he makes a halt, and, sometime, he travels. At one time, he

---

[8] *Ihya-ul-uloom*, vol. I, p. 243.

[9] Ibid., vol. I, p. 240.

pitches his tent, and, at another, he knocks it down. He is the slave of every nod, and gesture and does simply what he is called upon to do. He has no choice of his own. He has hardly halted at *mina* that he is required to move on to *arafat* but without breaking the journey at *muzdalifa.*

On reaching Arafat he engages himself in prayer throughout the day and when the sun has set, he finds himself tired and wanting to spend the night there but is commanded to proceed to Muzdalifa. He has been regular in prayer all his life but there he is told to forgo the Salat of Maghrib for he is the bondman of Allah, not of Salat or habit. The Salat he offers at Muzdalifa jointly with that of Isha. His stay at Muzdalifa is very pleasant and he wishes to prolong it, but it is not allowed to him, and he is bidden to leave for Mina.

The same was the practice of Hazrat Ibrahim and of all the Divine Apostles and men of faith and virtue, now travelling, now staying, now meeting, now parting, neither servile to desire nor yielding to caprice.

Time and Place

No other place could be more appropriate for it than Mecca where the forerunner of the votaries of faith and the most dearly loved bondman of God of his time had presented the most glowing tribute of devotion and sacrifice the world has ever known. All the Prophets of the Lord, monotheists and adorers of Divinity who came after him followed in his footsteps, emulated his example in every detail, and re-enacted the same story of fealty and love. They, in the same manner, circumambulated around the House of Ka'aba, performed the Saree between Safa and Marwa, encamped at Arafat, spent the night at Muzdalifa, threw the pebbles at Jemarat and offered the sacrifice of animals at Mina.

Thus, in time and space, in the chapters of the episode that is repeated over and over again, in the rites and formalities in which the example of Hazrat Ibrahim is followed, in the life-giving drafts of love from which the pilgrims draw new vitality, in the warmth of feeling and enthusiasm which envelops them entirely, in the company of diverse groups of Muslims which is available to them all the time, in the religious and spiritual congregation the like of which is not to be seen anywhere, and in the soulful melodies of prayer, supplication and repentance that fill the atmosphere constantly, that vital element, that indescribable quality is still present which infuses a new life, imparts a new keenness, instils a new hope and revives the languishing flame of love and evokes the Mercy of the Lord.

Many enlightened scholars of Islam have referred to the miraculous quality of this congregation of attracting the blessings of Allah and arousing the hearts, however insensitive they may have grown, and enkindling in them the feelings of devotion and earnestness. As Imam Ghazali, for instance, writes: "When the thoughts, hopes and aspirations are concentrated on a particular point, when the hearts are seized with eagerness, the hands are stretching towards Allah and the eyes are lifting towards the heavens, when everyone is, jointly and with full attention and solicitude, begging the Mercy of the Lord then, at that time, do not imagine that the Supreme Being will disappoint them, allow their exertions to go waste and keep them denied of His Favours."[10]

Hazrat Shah Waliullah, similarly, has said, "The fundamental principle of the Haj is that a large body of pious and virtuous servants got together at a particular time and recollected the state of those on whom was a special favour of Allah, such as the Prophets, the Truthful, the Duteous and the Martyrs, and at a place which abounded with the signs of the Almighty, the Gracious One, and where the meritorious and whole-souled representatives of the Ummat assembled, moved by reverence for the Landmarks of Allah., crying and beseeching, invoking His Aid and seeking His Forgiveness, because when the hearts beat in unison and people come together in this spirit there is no thriftiness in the bestowal of Mercy and Benevolence. The Prophet has said that Satan never feels more dejected, crestfallen and humiliated than on the day of Arafa."[11]

Hazrat Shah Waliullah goes on to say: "It is also a part of purification of the self that a man should break

---

[10] *Ihya-ul-Uloom*, Vol. I, p. 243.

[11] *Hujjatullah*, Vol. I, p. 59

his journey and stay at the places where the spiritually evolved and praiseworthy 'Friends of Allah' have been staying with reverence of the heart and uttermost devotion, filling the air with His Name. It will prove to be a source of nearness to the Angels and the Celestial World for men of virtue because when they stay there, they will also get dyed in the same hue."[12]

Renewal of Contact

One of the chief purposes of the Haj is the renewal of bond or contact with Hazrat Ibrahim, the founder *Millat-i-Hanifi*[13]. It affords a splendid opportunity to safeguard his legacy, to compare one's living with the way he had shown and to own way of take stock of the condition of Muslims with a view to improving it.

The Haj is a kind of annual concourse through which the Muslims can look into themselves, discover their faults and chalk out plans for their regeneration, and for ridding themselves of the influences they may

---

[12] Ibid.

[13] Denoting a community which is committed exclusively to God.

have accepted from peoples and communities among which they live.

In the words of Hazrat Shah Waliullah, "One of the objects of the Haj is the preservation of the legacy of Hazrat Ibrahim and Hazrat Ismail both of whom can be said to be the leaders of *Millat-i-Hanifi* and its founders in Arabia. The sacred Prophet, also, was raised up so that through him *Millat-i-Hanifi* gained ascendency in the world and was victorious.

﴿هُوَ ٱجْتَبَىٰكُمْ وَمَا جَعَلَ عَلَيْكُمْ فِى ٱلدِّينِ مِنْ حَرَجٍ ۚ مِّلَّةَ أَبِيكُمْ إِبْرَٰهِيمَ ۚ﴾

He ⌜Who⌝ has chosen you, and laid upon you no hardship in the religion—the way of your forefather Abraham. (22: 78).

It is, therefore, essential for us to protect the things we have received from the leader of this community as an inheritance, viz., personal characterists[14] and rituals

---

[14] The term includes ten items: the cutting (or trimming) of moustaches. the growing of the beard, the brushing of teeth with Miswak (twig), the cleaning of the nose with water, the cutting. of

of the Haj. As the Prophet once said, 'Stay at places set apart for the Haj for you are the inheritors of your father's legacy."[15]

Revivification of the Episode of Ibrahim

The most fascinating feature of the Haj is the spirit of enchantment, devotion and self-effacement which pervades the entire pilgrimage, from the beginning to the end. In it, the governance of the mind is entrusted to the heart and the glorious example of the earnest men of God and His genuine adorers, and their fore-runner, Hazrat Ibrahim, the Friend of Allah, is followed in every act and observance. Sometimes, the pilgrim walks zealously round the House of Ka'aba, sometimes, he kisses the Black Stone, and, sometimes, he portrays the intensity of mother's love at Safa and

---

the nails, the washing of the phalanges of fingers, the plucking of the hair of the armpits, the removal of the hair under the naval, the purification after a natural evacuation with water, and circumcision (-Reproduced from Abu Da'ud as related by Hazrat Ayesha). About the tenth item the narrator says that she was not sure whether it was circumcision or rinsing of mouth, but Qazi Ayaz and Imam Nawawi are definite that it was circumcision.

[15] *Hujjatullah*, Vol. 1, p. 42

Marwa by running where Hazrat Hajira, the mother of Hazrat Ismail, had run and walking with poise and dignity where she had walked in that way. Thereafter, he is bidden to leave for Mina on the 8th day of Zil-Hijja, and then, to stay in the valley of Arafat and devote himself earnestly to prayer and supplication. The night is spent at Muzdalifa, and, in the morning, he returns to Mina. All this is done solely and for no other reason than to emulate the example of Hazrat Ibrahim and the sacred Prophet.

The most striking part, however, of this unique display of love and emulation is the rite of Rami Jemar which is simply the simulation of an act performed by Hazrat Ibrahim, There is a force in following the example of the devout servants of the Lord which is catching.

The inner reliance of these glorious specimens of faith, their matchless spirit of love and dedication is trans- mitted to those who strive to follow in their footsteps like an electric current. It is the best and most effective way to attract the Mercy of the Lord. No spectacle is more enthralling for those who have experienced this feeling than the getting together of ardent adorers and faithful bondmen on that blessed land for re-enacting the magnificent episode and recreating the sublime events that had taken place thousands of years ago but have been eternalised by God and endowed with His gracious acceptance. It has been decreed by Him that His loyal and truthful servants, from all over the world, will re-enact the whole series of events in the same way and in the spirit of defeating and disgracing the Devil, fortifying and strengthening the faith and emulating the soul-stirring example of Hazrat Ibrahim.

Life-Story of Hazrat Ibrahim as Related in Quran

Hazrat Ibrahim was born in a leading family of priests at Urwa (now included in Iraq). Image-carving was the occupation of his ancestors who were also the keepers of the biggest temple in the town. His family was attached to that place of worship, both spiritually and professionally, and when faith gets mixed up with occupation and religious sentiment with economic self-interest, the situation invariably becomes very complex and delicate. In this atmosphere of gloom and rigidity, there was little to encourage the growth of true love and devotion to God or to move the people to rebel against the absurdity of polytheistic tenets and idolatrous practices. But with Hazrat Ibrahim whom God had chosen for Apostleship and the resuscitation of humanity it was different.

﴿وَلَقَدْ ءَاتَيْنَآ إِبْرَٰهِيمَ رُشْدَهُۥ مِن قَبْلُ وَكُنَّا بِهِۦ عَٰلِمِينَ ٥١﴾

And indeed, we had granted Abraham sound judgment early on, for We knew him well ⌜to be worthy of it⌝. (21: 51).

Hazrat Ibrahim launches his crusade against Ignorance from a stage where even most powerful revolutionary movements, generally, fail to make a headway. It was the stage of family, of the home in which a man is born and brought up and to which he is bound in loyalty and affection by innumerable ties. Now, all those things happen that have been related so eloquently in the Quran. These include the breaking of the idols by him, the consternation of the priests of the temple and their unbounded anger and revengefulness, the lighting up of a huge fire for this young and deep-hearted rebel, the cooling down of the fire and its turning into a source of peace and safety for him, and, finally, his forceful speech before the tyrant and straightforward replies to questions put to him in his Court.[16]

Hazrat Ibrahim's refusal to submit to the moral and spiritual perversion and depravity of his age evokes such a fearful response in the people of his town that they all turn against him. He is excluded from social fellowship and persecuted by the rulers. But this oppressive and spiteful treatment makes no impression upon him. He remains supremely unmoved as if it was just what he was looking forward to. Cheerfully and without rancour, he migrates from his birth-place because is not the real wealth, the wealth of faith, still in his possession, intact and undivided? He travels alone, without a friend or helper. Everywhere, on the way he meets the same type of people, the same prevalence of ignorance, idolatry, corruption and sensuality upon which he had turned his back. On arrival in Egypt, he is confronted with a grave situation but succeeds in leaving that country safely with his wife on whom its ruler had an evil eye.

---

[16] These happenings are described in detail in *Sura-i-Ambia*. (51-70).

Ultimately, he reaches Syria where he decides to stay for its climate is agreeable. Here, again, he takes up the mission of preaching the Oneness of God and denouncing idolatry with the same singleness of purpose. Hazrat Ibrahim takes a liking for Syria. It abounds in natural scenery; its soil is fertile, and its people are prosperous. But soon, he is bidden to go to another land which is just the opposite of it in richness and fertility. But he has no choice in the matter. He has no rights, only duties. He is but to obey, not to reason why. He has no preference for any country. The whole world is his homeland and the entire mankind his family. He is commanded to migrate from Syria with his wife, Hajir, and infant son.

Hazrat Ibrahim comes to a valley which is devoid of vegetation and surrounded on all sides by rugged mountains. Its climate is severe and it is also entirely uninhabited. There is no one in it who can be a source of solace and comfort. He is told to leave his helpless wife and child there and move away solely for the strength of faith in God and in compliance with His Command. He is required to do so in such a state that he is totally resigned to the Divine Will and there is not a trace of fear or hesitation in his heart, nor a shadow of doubt regarding the promise of his Lord. On the contrary, he is to act in defiance of all the dictates of reason and experience, and yet to remain steadfast, firm and unflinching, giving the fullest proof of reliance upon God and disregard of material means and resources when he is assailed with doubt or fear grips his heart.

After Hazrat Ibrahim has departed all those things happen, in the natural course, that were dreaded. The child becomes restless with thirst, and so does the mother. But where was water to be found in that dry, unoccupied land? There was not a drop of it in the whole valley. Overcome with anxiety and with the intensity of mother's love, Hazrat Hajir begins to run frantically between the two hills (of Safa and Marwa) in search of water and in the hope of meeting a caravan that may be passing that way. When she approaches the other hill, she is suddenly seized with fear about the safety of her child? Is it alive or has something happened to it? She hurries back to the child and assures herself that it was well. Then she again runs towards that hill, hoping against hope that she will come upon a traveller or find a source of water up there. She is worried and apprehensive: At the same time, she is calm and serene. She is a Prophet's wife and a Prophet's mother, but she does not believe in the futility of effort. She does not regard striving and the seeking of material means to be contrary to the spirit of faith and reliance on God. She is disturbed but not dejected. She has the utmost trust in God but there is no room in it for inaction. The world. has never seen such a spectacle before. The Providence, at last, is stirred and a spring bursts forth as if from nowhere. This is the blessed, ever flowing fountain of Zam Zam which neither dries up nor dwindles. It is sufficient for the whole of mankind and for all generations to come. The world has been drinking at it and will continue to do so till the end of time. There is propitiousness in it as well as health and a reward.

The Almighty has made the spontaneous act of a pious, believing lady a deliberate observance and prescribed it as a religious duty for everyone including kings and potentates, thinkers and scholars. Unless they perform the *Sa'ee* between the hills of Safa and Marwa their Haj will remain incomplete. The two points are, in fact, the destination of all devout souls and *Sa'ee* offers the aptest illustration of the viewpoint of a believer which combines both reason and emotion and faith and feeling. A believer makes a full use of his intellectual powers in his worldly needs but, sometimes, also gives a free rein to the emotional urges whose roots are deeper and stronger than those of thought. He lives in a world which is full of temptations. But like the pilgrim doing the *Sa'ee* between Safa and Marwa he passes quickly through it without being distracted. His heart is set on his destination. To him life is like the few turns he takes between the two hills in obedience to the Command of his Lord and in emulation of the example set by the pious precursors. His faith does not come in the way of critical study and investigation and his *Sa'ee* (exertion) offers no hindrance to trustfulness and reliance on God. It is an event whose worth and significance can be summed up in just two words: love and obedience.

The child (Ismail) grows up and attains the age when a father is drawn most lovingly to his offspring. He goes out with his father, runs with him and keeps his company in many ways. The loving and affectionate father is very fond of his son. And herein lie the seeds of crisis for his heart is a pure and noble heart which is reserved exclusively for the love of the Divine One. It is not anybody's heart but of the Friend of Allah. Love can put up with anything but a co-sharer. it cannot suffer a rival. When such is the case with human love what would Divine love be like? This is the position when inspiration comes to Hazrat Ibrahim that he should offer the sacrifice of his son. The dreams of the Prophets are in the nature of Divine revelations. Hence, when the suggestion is conveyed to him again and again, he knows in his heart that it is the Will of God which shall be done. He asks his son for without his consent the deed cannot be performed. The son remains steadfast. He gives a glittering proof of self-surrender. It could, of course, not be otherwise for was he himself not a Prophet, and the son and grandson of a Prophet?

﴿فَلَمَّا بَلَغَ مَعَهُ ٱلسَّعْىَ قَالَ يَٰبُنَىَّ إِنِّىٓ أَرَىٰ فِى ٱلْمَنَامِ أَنِّىٓ أَذْبَحُكَ فَٱنظُرْ مَاذَا تَرَىٰ ۚ قَالَ يَٰٓأَبَتِ ٱفْعَلْ مَا تُؤْمَرُ ۖ سَتَجِدُنِىٓ إِن شَآءَ ٱللَّهُ مِنَ ٱلصَّٰبِرِينَ ١٠٢﴾

Then when the boy reached the age to work with him, Abraham said, "O my dear son! I have seen in a dream that I ⌜must⌝ sacrifice you. So, tell me what you think." He replied, "O my dear father! Do as you are commanded. Allah willing, you will find me steadfast." (37: 102)

There, now, takes place a miraculous event that cannot be explained by any known natural law. Hazrat Ibrahim comes out with his beloved son. He is going to sacrifice the son at the Command of God, and the son, too, is accompanying him willingly. The goal before them is the same. It is in compliance with the Command of Allah and total resignation to His Will. In the way they are met by the Devil who is always eager to deceive man and deprive him of goodness and rectitude. He tries to dissuade them from carrying out their intention by presenting before them the alternative of the defiance of God in a most alluring manner and playing upon their natural weakness for life. But they do not listen to him and get ready for the supreme act of submission. The moment, finally, comes which is enough to afflict with agony not only men but even the djinn and angels. Hazrat Ibrahim lays his son on the ground, places the knife on his throat and proceeds to cut it. But the Will of God intervenes because what was intended was not the slaying of Hazrat Ismail but of the love that had come in the way of the love of Allah and begun to compete with it. That love had been killed with the placing of the knife on Hazrat Ismail's throat. Hazrat Ismail was born to live and to prosper and to raise up a lineage which was also to include the Last of the prophets. How could he be put to death before the fulfilment of his mission? God, therefore, sent down a ram, as a ransom for him, from the Heaven so that it may be slaughtered in his place and made it a religious ceremony to be observed by all the followers of Hazrat Ibrahim and their descendants. During the 'sacrificial days' of the Haj they revive the memory of the 'sublime sacrifice' and make an offering of their wealth to God by spending it in His way.

﴿فَلَمَّآ أَسْلَمَا وَتَلَّهُۥ لِلْجَبِينِ ١٠٣ وَنَـٰدَيْنَـٰهُ أَن يَـٰٓإِبْرَٰهِيمُ ١٠٤ قَدْ
صَدَّقْتَ ٱلرُّءْيَآ ۚ إِنَّا كَذَٰلِكَ نَجْزِى ٱلْمُحْسِنِينَ ١٠٥ إِنَّ هَـٰذَا لَهُوَ
ٱلْبَلَـٰٓؤُا۟ ٱلْمُبِينُ ١٠٦ وَفَدَيْنَـٰهُ بِذِبْحٍ عَظِيمٍ ١٠٧ وَتَرَكْنَا عَلَيْهِ فِى
ٱلْـَٔاخِرِينَ ١٠٨ سَلَـٰمٌ عَلَىٰٓ إِبْرَٰهِيمَ ١٠٩﴾

Then when they submitted ⌜to Allah's Will⌝, and Abraham laid him on the side of his forehead ⌜for sacrifice⌝, We called out to him, "O Abraham! You have already fulfilled the vision." Indeed, this is how We reward the good doers. That was truly a revealing test. And We ransomed his son with a great sacrifice, and blessed Abraham ⌜with honourable mention⌝ among later generations: "Peace be upon Abraham." (37: 103-109).

The incident which took place between Hazrat Ibrahim and Satan has also been immortalized by God and it has been decreed by Him that pebbles should be thrown where Satan stood in Hazrat Ibrahim's way and tried to dissuade him from carrying out the Divine Command. He has raised it to a ritual which has to be perform- ed during the most auspicious days of the Haj pilgrimage. The object is to produce a feeling of revulsion against Satan and to make it serve as an expression of defiance and resistance against him. The pilgrim draws a good deal of joy and inspiration from it provided that he is sound of faith and his understanding is correct and there is present in him a genuine desire to submit to the Divine Will. In re-enacting this part of the episode, he feels that he is engaged in a solemn struggle against the forces of evil in which the defeat of Satan is certain.

Years roll by on this event, the child has grown into a young man and the mantle of Apostleship has fallen upon him. The call of Hazrat Ibrahim has also, borne fruit and spread widely. It was now in need of a strong base which could lend support to the Divine faith and sustain it. There were innumerable temples and places in the world where Devil and the sensual appetites were freely worshipped. But on God's good earth there was, till then, not a place dedicated solely to His worship. Thus, now that the faith had taken root, and the foundations of *Ummat-i-Muslima*[17] were securely laid Hazrat Ibrahim was commanded to build the House of God which was to be the refuge of all mankind. Father and son together construct the sacred edifice which, though very simple and ordinary to look at, is full of grandeur and solidity from the point of view of object. They both carry stones and raise its walls.

﴿وَإِذۡ يَرۡفَعُ إِبۡرَٰهِـۧمُ ٱلۡقَوَاعِدَ مِنَ ٱلۡبَيۡتِ وَإِسۡمَٰعِيلُ رَبَّنَا
تَقَبَّلۡ مِنَّآۖ إِنَّكَ أَنتَ ٱلسَّمِيعُ ٱلۡعَلِيمُ ١٢٧ رَبَّنَا وَٱجۡعَلۡنَا

[17] Denoting the community of the faithful.

مُسْلِمَيْنِ لَكَ وَمِن ذُرِّيَّتِنَآ أُمَّةً مُّسْلِمَةً لَّكَ وَأَرِنَا مَنَاسِكَنَا وَتُبْ عَلَيْنَآ إِنَّكَ أَنتَ ٱلتَّوَّابُ ٱلرَّحِيمُ ﴿١٢٨﴾

And ⌜remember⌝ when Abraham raised the foundation of the House with Ishmael, ⌜both praying,⌝ "Our Lord! Accept ⌜this⌝ from us. You are indeed the All-Hearing, All-Knowing. Our Lord! Make us both ⌜fully⌝ submit to You[1] and from our descendants a nation that will submit to You. Show us our rituals, and turn to us in grace. You are truly the Accepter of Repentance, Most Merciful. (2: 127-8)

The House was raised on the foundations of matchless faith and single-minded devotion. The Almighty God bestowed His choicest acceptance upon it and endued it with permanence. He endowed it with inner as well as outward elegance, made it *Qibla-gah*[18] of the world and caused for it a unique and undying attraction in the hearts. It draws people from all parts of the world like a magnet. They flock to it with rare enthusiasm and reverence and make an offering of their heart and soul to it. It is free from external adornments

---

[18] The place one turns to when at prayer.

and artificial decorations, and it is situated at a place which is removed from the broad stream of life and the din and clang of civilisation. Yet there is something about it, which is overwhelming, irresistible.

When the house was ready, a voice came from the Great Beyond. It spoke:

﴿وَأَذِّن فِي ٱلنَّاسِ بِٱلۡحَجِّ يَأۡتُوكَ رِجَالٗا وَعَلَىٰ كُلِّ ضَامِرٖ يَأۡتِينَ
مِن كُلِّ فَجٍّ عَمِيقٖ ٢٧ لِّيَشۡهَدُواْ مَنَٰفِعَ لَهُمۡ وَيَذۡكُرُواْ ٱسۡمَ
ٱللَّهِ فِيٓ أَيَّامٖ مَّعۡلُومَٰتٍ عَلَىٰ مَا رَزَقَهُم مِّنۢ بَهِيمَةِ ٱلۡأَنۡعَٰمِۖ
فَكُلُواْ مِنۡهَا وَأَطۡعِمُواْ ٱلۡبَآئِسَ ٱلۡفَقِيرَ ٢٨ ثُمَّ لۡيَقۡضُواْ تَفَثَهُمۡ
وَلۡيُوفُواْ نُذُورَهُمۡ وَلۡيَطَّوَّفُواْ بِٱلۡبَيۡتِ ٱلۡعَتِيقِ ٢٩﴾

Call ⌜all⌝ people to the pilgrimage. They will come to you on foot and on every lean camel from every distant path, so they may obtain the benefits ⌜in store⌝ for them and pronounce the Name of Allah on appointed days over the sacrificial animals He has provided for them. So, eat from their meat and feed the desperately poor. (22: 27-29)

At the time of Hazrat Ibrahim the world was a slave to the operation of the law of cause and effect and people had begun to place an excessive reliance on material aids and resources. It was imagined that causes were absolute and independent in themselves, and a new kind of fetishism had come upside by side with traditional idolatry. The life of Hazrat Ibrahim was a revolt against these very 'image-carvers' and 'idol-worshippers'. It was a call to pure Monotheism, to unqualified belief in the Power of God with all its immensity and boundless- ness. It was a declaration of truth that He alone was the Creator of all things, the Prime Mover, the Causer of causes, the real Lord and Master, who, when He pleased, separated the causes from their origins and altered the properties of things. He took away from a thing what was peculiar to it and brought forth from it an effect that was supposed to be dissimilar. He made use of whatever He liked and in whatever way He pleased.

The people had prepared a fire for Hazrat Ibrahim, and they cried:

﴿قَالُواْ حَرِّقُوهُ وَٱنصُرُوٓاْ ءَالِهَتَكُمۡ إِن كُنتُمۡ فَٰعِلِينَ ٦٨﴾

They concluded, “Burn him up to avenge your gods, if you must act.” (21: 68)

But Hazrat Ibrahim knew that the fire was subservient to the Will of Allah. To burn was not an absolute characteristic of it which could not be taken away but only a relative attribute that had been placed in it by God as a trust. Its control and operation lay wholly in His hands who could transform it into a flowerbed in the twinkling of an eye. With this faith and conviction Hazrat Ibrahim jumped into the fire and it turned out to be exactly as he had expected.

﴿قُلْنَا يَٰنَارُ كُونِي بَرْدًا وَسَلَٰمًا عَلَىٰٓ إِبْرَٰهِيمَ ٦٩ وَأَرَادُوا۟ بِهِۦ
كَيْدًا فَجَعَلْنَٰهُمُ ٱلْأَخْسَرِينَ ٧٠﴾

We ordered, “O fire! Be cool and safe for Abraham!” They had sought to harm him, but We made them the worst losers. (21: 69-70)

Life was commonly believed to be dependent upon water, fields and orchards. People used to be on the lookout for regions to make their home that were suitable for themselves as well as for their gods, where there was an abundant supply of water, the soil was rich and facilities for trade and industry were easily obtainable.

But Hazrat Ibrahim acted differently. In utter disregard of the biddings of intellect and experience, he chose for his small family of a wife and son a dry and barren valley where not a blade of grass grew, and which was also completely cut off from the outside world and separated from the areas of prosperity. On arriving there he prayed to Allah to enlarge the provision of his posterity, to incline the hearts of men towards them and to provide them with all kinds of fruit without any apparent means.

﴿رَّبَّنَآ إِنِّيٓ أَسۡكَنتُ مِن ذُرِّيَّتِي بِوَادٍ غَيۡرِ ذِي زَرۡعٍ عِندَ بَيۡتِكَ ٱلۡمُحَرَّمِ رَبَّنَا لِيُقِيمُواْ ٱلصَّلَوٰةَ فَٱجۡعَلۡ أَفۡـِٔدَةٗ مِّنَ ٱلنَّاسِ تَهۡوِيٓ إِلَيۡهِمۡ وَٱرۡزُقۡهُم مِّنَ ٱلثَّمَرَٰتِ لَعَلَّهُمۡ يَشۡكُرُونَ ٣٧﴾

Our Lord! I have settled some of my offspring in a barren valley, near Your Sacred House, our Lord, so that they may establish prayer. So, make the hearts of ⌜believing⌝

people incline towards them and provide them with fruits, so perhaps they will be thankful. (14: 37)

The prayer was granted by Allah, and in what a magnificent manner! Both peace and sustenance were assured to his succeeding generations and the valley of Mecca was made the home of fruits and his other bounties.

﴿وَقَالُوٓاْ إِن نَّتَّبِعِ ٱلۡهُدَىٰ مَعَكَ نُتَخَطَّفۡ مِنۡ أَرۡضِنَآۚ أَوَلَمۡ نُمَكِّن لَّهُمۡ حَرَمًا ءَامِنًا يُجۡبَىٰٓ إِلَيۡهِ ثَمَرَٰتُ كُلِّ شَيۡءٖ رِّزۡقًا مِّن لَّدُنَّا وَلَٰكِنَّ أَكۡثَرَهُمۡ لَا يَعۡلَمُونَ ٥٧﴾

They say ⌜to the Prophet⌝, "If we were to follow ⌜true⌝ guidance with you, we would certainly be snatched away from our land." Have We not established for them a safe haven ⌜in Mecca⌝ to which fruits of all kinds are brought as a provision from Us? But most of them do not know ⌜this favour⌝. (28: 57)

﴿فَلۡيَعۡبُدُواْ رَبَّ هَٰذَا ٱلۡبَيۡتِ ٣ ٱلَّذِيٓ أَطۡعَمَهُم مِّن جُوعٖ وَءَامَنَهُم مِّنۡ خَوۡفِۢ ٤﴾

let them worship the Lord of this ⌜Sacred⌝ House, who has fed them against hunger and made them secure against fear. (106: 3-4)

Hazrat Ibrahim had abandoned his family at a place where not a drop of water was to be found but Allah caused a spring to spout forth from the parched, stony land. Water began to gush, from the sand, all by itself, and, even to this day, it has been going on like that, without an interruption. People drink it and take it home in barrels. He had left his wife and son in a desolate and uninhabited valley but soon it began to hum with people drawn from every nook and corner of the world. Hazrat Ibrahim's life was a challenge to the exaggerated materialism and blind submission to the law of cause and effect of his age, and an affirmation of faith in the Omnipotence and All-powerfulness of God- and it is the unchanging practice of the Lord that He makes means and resources subordinate to faith and produces results from them as are outside the range of human understanding.

Renewal of the Call of Hazrat Ibrahim

The Haj along with its rituals and the events to which these are related, the robe of indifference to material phenomena and liberation from conceit and vainglory which the pilgrim puts on and the rites of *Waqoof*,[19] *Ifaza*,[20] *Rajm*[21], *Sa'ee*; and Tawaf he performs are, in fact, a means to the promotion and activisation in his life of the values and concepts of Monotheism, negation of material causes, reliance on God, Divine propitiation and making sacrifices in His way. All these events, formalities and observances typify an open rejection of customary behaviour and a revival of the spirit of faith, love and surrender. The Haj holds a guarantee to the preservation of these lofty ideals, sublime sentiments and priceless moral and spiritual values and of the unmatched Islamic conception of human equality and brotherhood which transcends all national, political and geographical barriers. It is a call for following the example of Hazrat Ibrahim, for producing the spirit of

---

[19] The stay at Arafat between the mid-day of the 9th and the early hours of the 10th of Zil-Hijja.

[20] Return to Mecca from Mina.

[21] The throwing of pebbles at the Jemaras.

his faith and devotion in ourselves and for holding aloft his teachings everywhere and at all times.

﴿وَجَٰهِدُواْ فِي ٱللَّهِ حَقَّ جِهَادِهِۦۚ هُوَ ٱجۡتَبَىٰكُمۡ وَمَا جَعَلَ
عَلَيۡكُمۡ فِي ٱلدِّينِ مِنۡ حَرَجٖۚ مِّلَّةَ أَبِيكُمۡ إِبۡرَٰهِيمَۚ هُوَ
سَمَّىٰكُمُ ٱلۡمُسۡلِمِينَ مِن قَبۡلُ وَفِي هَٰذَا لِيَكُونَ ٱلرَّسُولُ
شَهِيدًا عَلَيۡكُمۡ وَتَكُونُواْ شُهَدَآءَ عَلَى ٱلنَّاسِۚ فَأَقِيمُواْ
ٱلصَّلَوٰةَ وَءَاتُواْ ٱلزَّكَوٰةَ وَٱعۡتَصِمُواْ بِٱللَّهِ هُوَ مَوۡلَىٰكُمۡۖ فَنِعۡمَ
ٱلۡمَوۡلَىٰ وَنِعۡمَ ٱلنَّصِيرُ ٧٨﴾

Strive for ⌜the cause of⌝ Allah in the way He deserves, for ⌜it is⌝ He ⌜Who⌝ has chosen you and laid upon you no hardship in the religion—the way of your forefather Abraham. ⌜It is Allah⌝ Who named you 'the ones who submit'[1] ⌜in the⌝ earlier ⌜Scriptures⌝ and in this ⌜Quran⌝, so that the Messenger may be a witness over you, and that you may be witnesses over humanity. So, establish prayer, pay alms-tax, and hold fast to Allah. He ⌜alone⌝ is your Guardian. What an excellent Guardian, and what an excellent Helper! (22: 78)

A New Chapter

The call of Hazrat Ibrahim marks the beginning of a new chapter in the story of our race. It draws a line of separation between one current of history and another. The whole of mankind gets divided into two camps that remain permanently in a state of war with each other: with it the old era ends and the new begins. Hazrat Ibrahim was favoured by God with an eternal call and an everlasting Ummat and Apostleship: spiritual guidance and religious leadership were, forever, decreed for his descendants. For his followers it was ordained for all times that they will shoulder the responsibility of carrying out the struggle against the forces of evil and perform the task of the preaching and propagation of faith. The duty of guiding humanity to its ultimate destination and protecting the light of faith against the onslaughts of darkness and sensuality was now going to be theirs.

Hope of Humanity

The Haj pilgrimage, the annual congregation of the followers of Hazrat Ibrahim at Mecca, and the rites and ceremonies connected with it, possess in full measure the capacity to forge a living contact among his spiritual heirs and successors and impart a new life to the aims and ideals indicated above.

﴿۞ جَعَلَ ٱللَّهُ ٱلْكَعْبَةَ ٱلْبَيْتَ ٱلْحَرَامَ قِيَـٰمًا لِّلنَّاسِ وَٱلشَّهْرَ ٱلْحَرَامَ وَٱلْهَدْىَ وَٱلْقَلَـٰٓئِدَ ۚ ذَٰلِكَ لِتَعْلَمُوٓا۟ أَنَّ ٱللَّهَ يَعْلَمُ مَا فِى ٱلسَّمَـٰوَٰتِ وَمَا فِى ٱلْأَرْضِ وَأَنَّ ٱللَّهَ بِكُلِّ شَىْءٍ عَلِيمٌ ﴿٩٧﴾﴾

Allah has made the Ka'bah—the Sacred House—a sanctuary of well-being for all people, along with the sacred months, the sacrificial animals, and the ⌜offerings decorated with⌝ garlands. All this so you may know that Allah knows whatever is in the heavens and whatever is on the earth, and that He has ⌜perfect⌝ knowledge of everything. (5: 97)

Eternal Home of Religious Guidance and Endeavour

During the Islamic era and the ministry of the Prophet Mohammad the House of Allah in Mecca, where the rites of the Haj are performed, became permanent home of religious guidance and true spirituality. Here the cold cellar of the heart is warmed up again, and the World of Islam rallies to it, year after year, to pay the tribute of love and submission and give a marvellous demonstration of its attachment to this pillar of faith. The greatest of rulers, plutocrats, scholars, and divines walk around it in an exalted state of feeling but not unbounded by reason and awareness. They furnish a practical proof of the fact that they are united in spite of the things that apparently divide them, bound to each other in spite of mutual strife and dissensions, and strong in spite of widespread poverty and backwardness. Though the Muslims are scattered all over the world and engrossed in their own problems and difficulties and divided into various races and nationalities they become one at a particular point where all their divergences, strife and contentions disappear, and they are moulded into a compact whole. Their life, in the pilgrimage, consists wholly of faith and belief, worship and oblation and *Tawaf* and *Sa'ee*, and their only halts are at Mina and Arafat and at such other places where the rites of the Haj are to be performed. They are constantly on the move, advancing towards their goal, meeting new people, traversing new paths and discovering new dimensions. The journey within journey continues till they depart from the world and go to meet their Maker.

Town of the Beloved

It is natural for a Muslim, especially if he has come from a distant land, to want to go to Medina, after he has completed the Haj, which had been the home of the sacred Prophet after migration and where his last resting place lies. Simply and sincerely, he is seized with the longing to betake himself to it and see the hallowed mosque from which emanated the rays of light that illumined the world and flowed out the springs of knowledge and spirituality which transformed it into a blooming garden. It was here that Islam took shelter in the days of tyranny and oppression and the initial chapters of its history were written. The soil of this wonderful city is soaked with the blood and tears of the holy Companions. It is but to be expected of the pilgrim that he desired keenly to offer prayers in the Mosque of the Prophet, one *Rak'at* of which is equal to thousand *Rak'ats* offered elsewhere[22], and to stay at places where the pious precursors, the martyrs and the truthful used to stay. He is hopeful of receiving from there some part

---

[22] It is related by Abu Huraira that the Prophet once said "A Rak'at of Salat in my mosque is equal to a thousand Rak'ats offered in any other mosque, save Masjid-i-Haram (the Grand Mosque of Mecca)."

of the celestial wealth of faith, earnestness and love, and of the courage to lay down his life in the cause of Islam. He is also inspired by the wish to send blessings on the holy Prophet through whom he was fortunate enough to obtain deliverance from Ignorance, to pass from the bondage of fellowmen to the bondage of God and to taste the sweetness of faith, and to realize the worth and dignity of man.

Protection against Pollution and Distortion

The Haj plays a vital role in the protection of the spiritual roots of the Muslim Millet. Nothing is more efficacious in keeping the Islamic faith safe from pollution, confusion, and distortion and the Ummat bound to its moorings and in dispelling the deceptions and subverting the conspiracies (which have led to the ruination of many a community in the past) than this annual congregation. Thanks to it, and the rites and formalities that are peculiar to it, the Muslim Millet, on the whole, is still inspired by the ideals associated with Hazrat Ibrahim (and which can be described as simplicity, profundity, uprightness, fidelity, tenderness, love and dedication) and has kept alive the tradition of passing on its legacy to the future generation. In this way it is like a throbbing, pulsating heart which is incessantly supplying new blood to the veins and arteries of the Ummat. The Haj affords an excellent opportunity of self-examination to the Muslims. They can test themselves on the anvil of the Ibrahimi origin and their leaders and reformers can take advantage of this unique combination of circumstances to purge them of the corrupting influence of the hypocrites, deceivers and extremists. Through it the Millet can safeguard its religious, cultural and intellectual identity and ward off the challenges of the narrow nationalism and parochialism that are inimical to the fundamental spirit of Islam and destructive of the organic unity of the spiritual heirs and successors of Hazrat Ibrahim.

The Muslims live under different conditions in different parts of the world. They pass through diverse phases of existence like activity and stagnation, affluence and want, peace and turmoil and ease and difficulty. Sometimes, they are plagued with problems relating to culture and civilisation, and, sometimes, political and material considerations put them on trial. At one place the government under which they live is progressive and benevolent, at another, it is reactionary and despotic.

But whatever the circumstances, the need is always there for the spark of faith in them to be stirred, the sentiment of love to be aroused and the lesson of unity and self- sacrifice to be imparted. God had made the Haj a spring- time in which the ever-green tree of the Ummat sends forth new blossoms and the universal fraternity of Islam re-asserts itself.

In the words of Hazrat Shah Waliullah: "Just as for the government it is necessary to hold a periodical survey so that it can be known who is loyal and who is disloyal and who is a conscientious worker and who is a shirker, and also that, through it, its power and authority may increase and the people and officials come close to each other the Ummat, too, stands in need of the Haj in order that the truthful may be separated from the hypocrites and people may come in ranks to the *durbar*[23] of Allah; they may know each-other and profit from each-other's company for better and more

[23] The place where formal gatherings are held by a sovereign.

desirable things are, generally, acquired by knowing and associating with one another.

Since the Haj is an occasion on which people come together it serves as an effective protection against sinful customs and practices, nothing can compare with it where recalling the state of the leaders and mentors of the Ummat and engendering the urge for emulating their example are concerned."[24]

At another place the distinguished scholar remarks,[25] "Included among the objects of the Haj is the one for which governments hold fairs and exhibitions. People come from far and near to see them, they meet one an- other and learn about the precepts of their State and pay their respects to its hallowed places. In the same way, the Haj is the fair or exhibition of Muslims in which a display of their glory is made, their energies are pooled together and the name of their community shines in the world. It is stated in the Quran:

﴿وَإِذْ جَعَلْنَا ٱلْبَيْتَ مَثَابَةً لِّلنَّاسِ وَأَمْنًا﴾

[24] *Hujjatullah*, Vol. I, pp. 59-60.

[25] Ibid., Vol. II, p. 42.

And ⌜remember⌝ when We made the Sacred House a centre and a sanctuary for the people. (2: 125)

Centre of Universal Guidance

It is the Will of Allah that even at most critical times the Haj will not be without the presence of the blessed personalities we speak of as 'doctors of divinity' 'favourites of the Divine Court', 'people of preaching and reform' and 'men of the inner world', It is on account of their participation that the atmosphere surrounding the Pilgrimage gets so overwhelmingly charged with radiance and spirituality that even the hardest of the hearts melt, the rebels and renegades are inclined to be repentant, the eyes that had never been moist with love or fear of God are flooded with tears, the cold furnaces of the hearts are lit up once again, the Mercy of the Lord descends from the heavens, the feeling of peace and tranquillity permeates the entire congregation and the Devil finds no place to hide his head. It is stated in the Traditions that "the Devil has never been seen more miserable, angry and downcast than on the Day of Arafa and it is so because he sees with his own eyes that the Mercy of the Lord is descending upon the earth and grievous sins are being forgiven."

There is an indescribable quality about the spiritual climate of the Haj. Muslims coming from faraway places experience an extraordinary awakening of the heart and they take back with them a provision of faith, love and enlightenment which sustains them and enables them to resist the pressures of fear, greed and lust. On their return, they also share it with their brothers who could not make the Pilgrimage owing to poverty, illness or any other valid reason and this wealth of religious feeling and awareness, thus, gains currency in the entire Islamic society, the illiterate and the unknowing feel encouraged to acquire the knowledge of faith, the weak and the downtrodden draw inspiration from it, the spirits of the dejected and the heart-sick are revived and the Ummat acquires a new strength to carry out the duty of preaching and guidance.

Demonstration of Islamic Equality and Fraternity

The Haj is a victory for Islamic nationalism over racial, linguistic or territorial nationalism for which a large number of Muslim countries also have, unfortunately, fallen. It is a proclamation as well as a most impressive manifestation of Islamic nationalism. On reaching there, the Muslims cast away their national or local garments which differentiate them from one another and to which some of them have become attached to the extent of being clannish and parochial, and put on the national robe of Islam, called Ihram, and they all sing the same song of humbleness and submission.

O God! Here I am! Here I am in Thy presence! Thou hast no partner! Here I am! All praise is for Thee and from Thee are all blessings! To Thee alone belongs Power and Rule Thou art without partner!

The rulers and the ruled, the masters and the slaves, the rich and the poor, the high and the low-all become one. The distinctions of class, race and geography lose their validity in their midst. The nationality of Islam transcends their whole existence. It is apparent from their apparel as well as watchword. It is the same with all the other formalities, prayers and rituals of the Haj in which people belonging to different lands and nationalities join one another and all the things that separate the near the remote, the Arab from the non-Arab, disappear at a single stroke into oblivion. They run together between the two hills of Safa and Marwa, travel together to Mina, betake themselves together to Arafat, pray together at *Jabal-i-Rahmat* (the Mount of Mercy) and spend the night together at Muzdalifa.

﴿فَإِذَآ أَفَضۡتُم مِّنۡ عَرَفَٰتٖ فَٱذۡكُرُواْ ٱللَّهَ عِندَ ٱلۡمَشۡعَرِ ٱلۡحَرَامِۖ وَٱذۡكُرُوهُ كَمَا هَدَىٰكُمۡ وَإِن كُنتُم مِّن قَبۡلِهِۦ لَمِنَ ٱلضَّآلِّينَ ١٩٨﴾

When you return from 'Arafât, praise Allah near the sacred place and praise Him for having guided you, for surely before this ⌜guidance⌝ you were astray. (2: 198)

﴿ثُمَّ أَفِيضُواْ مِنۡ حَيۡثُ أَفَاضَ ٱلنَّاسُ وَٱسۡتَغۡفِرُواْ ٱللَّهَۚ إِنَّ ٱللَّهَ غَفُورٞ رَّحِيمٞ ١٩٩﴾

Then go forth with the rest of the pilgrims. And seek Allah's forgiveness. Surely Allah is All-Forgiving, Most Merciful. (2: 199)

They stay at Mina in a body and perform the rites of *Naher* (sacrificing of animals), *Halq* (shaving of the head) and *Rami* (throwing of pebbles) in each other's company.

As long as the Haj endures (and, Insha Allah, it will endure till the end of time) the cult of nationalism and other un-Islamic movements shall not succeed in swallowing up the Muslims. The Muslims will never give in to them, and in their countries (to which they are naturally attached) no other Ka'aba will, at any time, be set up which took the place of the Haj and became the centre of attraction for the whole of Muslims. The Qibla shall always remain one to which the Muslims of the East and the West will turn their faces. So also, will the House of Allah be forever one to which the Indian and the Afghan and the European and the American Muslims will be coming for the Haj Pilgrimage year after year.

﴿وَإِذْ جَعَلْنَا ٱلْبَيْتَ مَثَابَةً لِّلنَّاسِ وَأَمْنًا وَٱتَّخِذُوا۟ مِن مَّقَامِ إِبْرَٰهِـۧمَ مُصَلًّى﴾

And ⌜remember⌝ when We made the Sacred House[1] a centre and a sanctuary for the people ⌜saying⌝, "⌜You may⌝ take the standing-place of Abraham[2] as a site of prayer." (2: 125)

Benefits

The Haj has many other benefits, some of which are known to us, and some are not. Perhaps the benefits we do not know are more numerous than those we know. Eminent scholars of Islam have drawn attention to the benefits of the Haj that are hidden from our view. A verse of Sura-i-Haj of the Qur'an reads:

﴿لِّيَشۡهَدُواْ مَنَٰفِعَ لَهُمۡ﴾

So, they may obtain the benefits ⌜in store⌝ for them. (22: 28)

Here the word *Manafe* (of benefit) has been used in a general sense, ostensibly with the object of indicating the abundance of the advantages accruing from the Haj and their different categories and phases at different periods of time.[26]

---

[26] The Haj is an occasion on which the Muslims from all over the world come together and avail themselves of the things that are of benefit to them in various ways, they can take advantage of it to meet each other and discuss their problems. But this is not the real significance of the Haj as some of the present-day writers try to

show. The Haj is not in the nature of a political conference. whatever these self-appointed exponents of Islam may say. Were it so, the Haj would be held in a peaceful atmosphere with all the pilgrims staying at one place. This, naturally, would have facilitated deliberations. But the rites of the Pilgrimage are such that the Hajis have always to be on the move and there is little opportunity for them to sit together and confer. Moreover, had the Haj really been intended to be something of a Muslim conference on international affairs it would have been open only to leaders of Muslim opinion in various countries or, at least, special stress would have been laid on their presence while, in fact, it has been made obligatory for every Muslim, man or woman, who possesses the means to make the Pilgrimage and the obligation holds good for only once in a lifetime. It is not that a worldly advantage can or should not be derived from the Haj but that does not form a part of its fundamental aim and purpose. The Qur'an says:

﴿وَلِلَّهِ عَلَى ٱلنَّاسِ حِجُّ ٱلْبَيْتِ مَنِ ٱسْتَطَاعَ إِلَيْهِ سَبِيلًا ۚ وَمَن كَفَرَ فَإِنَّ ٱللَّهَ غَنِيٌّ عَنِ ٱلْعَٰلَمِينَ ﴿٩٧﴾﴾

Pilgrimage to this House is an obligation by Allah upon whoever is able among the people. And whoever disbelieves, then surely Allah is not in need of ⌜any of His⌝ creation. (3: 97)

A Tradition of the Prophet reads; "A person whom God has given enough to perform the Haj, if he fails to do so then it does not matter whether he dies a Jew or Christian."

The City of Peace should present a True Picture of the Islamic way of Life

The Haj is an annual congregation in which the Muslims from all parts of the world participate. They collect in one place, on a single platform, with a definite aim and conviction, and in a rare religious and spiritual atmosphere, and from it, they draw fresh strength and gain new inspiration. It gives them a splendid opportunity to remove the faults that may have crept into their beliefs and practices under the influence of alien ideologies and un-Islamic civilisations or as a result of imitating the ways of life pursued in the neighbouring countries, and to acquire the knowledge and awareness of faith from the 'fountain of purity' which is eternally protected against pollution and defilement. It is, therefore, essential both logically and from the point of view of the spirit of Islam and the Haj that the City of Peace (i.e., Mecca) with which the whole of the Pilgrimage is associated preserved the heritage of the Islamic programme of life in all its aspects and

---

If the Haj was to be an International Islamic Conference its form and design would have been different, and it would also not be held at such a remote and barren place.

presented such a picture of it that the pilgrims were able to appreciate its distinctiveness and to live through it, however brief their stay might be, is a reality. God has made the blessed city of Mecca the seat of the Haj and the place of refuge for all Muslims. They come here with the impression that it is the spiritual capital of Islam and the springhead of sanctity. On coming here an ordinary Muslim who lives far away from the nerve-centre of Islam regards everything related to it to be authentic. Whatever he sees or hears is to him the last word in correctness and propriety for the simple reason that in the eyes of the common Muslim the conduct of no one can be more in keeping with the standard of Islam than that of the people of Mecca and Medina. It could simply be no other way because the followers of every religion or civilisation look to its place of origin or spiritual or cultural headquarters for inspiration and believe what obtains there to be the measuring yard of excellence. Thus the lexicon of the Quraish is considered to be of the highest merit in Arabia, and next to it is the language of the Bedouin which sets the pattern for the idiom, pronunciation and mode of expression among the Arabs, Similarly, the conduct of the people of Medina was regarded as decisive in the Maliki school of

Jurisprudence and during the heyday of Spain the behaviour of the inhabitants of Cardova was held to be the standard of perfection by the jurists of the West. People, indeed, have always been in the habit of imagining the capitals of their countries to be the citadels of culture. They vie with each other in following the trends set over there in dress and other fields of personal and social behaviour. It is, therefore, a most disconcerting experience for Muslim religious teachers when pilgrims returning from the Seat of Islam tell them that what they had seen there was quite different from what they had been preaching.[27]

Distinctiveness

What is more important is that Mecca (the City of Peace) should in all circumstances uphold the standards of simplicity and austerity that brought the pilgrims closer to the social and spiritual climate in which the Muslims of the earliest centuries of Islam performed the Haj. On entering it, they should feel that

---

[27] The above passage is an abridgement of the speech delivered by the author at the Annual Conference of *Rabita-i-'Alam-i-Islami* held at Mecca in 1964.

they had stepped into a new world and were living in entirely different surroundings. This will inspire them to cast away the shadow of their past existence and imbibe new values. They will then, derive a rare spiritual satisfaction from their stay in that blessed town which they could never feel in their own homeland. On the other hand, if the House of Ka'aba or the *Haram Sharif*[28] remained true to their original state but their surroundings underwent a radical change and the town of Mecca and its neighbouring areas began to look like a part of Europe or America and the Western Civilisation, with all its virtues and vices swept over it and the Haji, who in the Shariat is described as the dishevelled and the dust laden', set about to enjoy thoroughly the luxuries of the modern age and lead a life of ease and comfort, he will not be able to feel the full moral and spiritual impact of the Pilgrimage.

The Haj, because of it, has been described as a kind of Jehad. It is related by Hazrat Ayesha that the Prophet once said. "The best and most superior Jehad is the Haj which finds acceptance (with God)." It is also related by

---

[28] The sacred enclosure of Mecca.

her that once she said to the Prophet that when Jehad was regarded to be a superior act why should they not engage in it (instead of performing the Haj)? The Prophet replied, "But a better kind of Jehad is the Haj on which there is the favour of the Lord." Another Tradition related by Hazrat Omar reads, "Make preparations for the Haj for it, too, is Jehad."

If, therefore, Mecca itself changes beyond recognition and accepts blindly the influence of the Western Civilisation and various modern contrivances of comfort and luxury are freely made available during the Haj the pilgrims will naturally be haunted by a sense of spiritual vacuum and a clear decline in the benefits of the Haj will take place on all sides.

Provisions of the Shariat

The holy law has provided the Haj with an environment which is basically conducive to self-realisation and inner upliftment. It has encompassed it with worship and endowed it with sanctity and spirituality. The journey of the Haj, for most people, is long and tedious. In it they have to pass through many lands and undergo diverse experiences. Temptations beset their path, business worries and other vexations tax their minds; they stop at strange places and come into contact with all sorts of people. Sometimes, they are also accompanied by their families which often proves to be an additional distraction. All these things can undermine the spirit of devotion and endeavour which holds the key to the blessedness of the Haj. There was, thus, not an inconsiderable danger of the Haj Pilgrimage getting reduced to another journey with the pilgrims going out as tourists and returning home empty-handed.

As a safeguard against it the Shariat has given to the Haj a colour of sanctity and sublimity that never fades. It has provided it with a built-in mechanism that allows neither neglect nor apathy nor any other vain or frivolous element to enter into it and ruin its beauty. The Shariat has laid down wise and comprehensive rules for the Haj which strengthen its hold on life and ensure its continuance as a most important means of correction and reform and of gaining access to God. To begin with. it has declared it to be the fourth fundamental duty in Islam and made it obligatory for all Muslims who fulfil certain conditions.

﴿وَلِلَّهِ عَلَى ٱلنَّاسِ حِجُّ ٱلْبَيْتِ مَنِ ٱسْتَطَاعَ إِلَيْهِ سَبِيلًاۚ وَمَن كَفَرَ فَإِنَّ ٱللَّهَ غَنِيٌّ عَنِ ٱلْعَٰلَمِينَ ٩٧﴾

Pilgrimage to this House is an obligation by Allah upon whoever is able among the people.[1] And whoever disbelieves, then surely Allah is not in need of ⌜any of His⌝ creation. (3: 97)

It is related by Hazrat Ali that the Prophet once said, "A person whom God has given enough to perform the Haj, if he fails to do so then it does not matter whether he dies a Jew or a Christian." Another Tradition of the holy Prophet reads: The foundation of Islam rests on these five pillars: The affirmation that there is no God save one God and Mohammad is His Apostle, the establishment of Salat, the payment of Zakat, the observance of Saum in the month of Ramadhan and the performance of the Haj by those who can afford to make the pilgrimage."

In the Traditions the virtues of the Haj and the high place it occupies in the sight of God have been stressed over and over again with the object of arousing the sentiments of faith and eagerness because unless these two sentiments are associated with an act, and it is motivated primarily by them God has no use for it. It is related by Hazrat Abu Huraira that the Prophet once said, "The reward for a pure and untainted Haj is Paradise itself and nothing short of it." In another Tradition related by him it is said that "he who performs the Haj and commits no lustful act during it and does not disobey God (in any other way), he will return from it as pure and sinless as he was at the time of his birth." Yet another Tradition of the holy Prophet reads, "Perform the Haj and the Umra for they both remove the sins in the same way as the furnace removes the impurities of gold, silver and iron, and there is no lesser recompense on a pure and untainted Haj than Paradise, and when a believer puts on the Ihram all his sins disappear with the setting of the sun." It is, further, related by Hazrat Ayesha that the Prophet once said: "On no other day does God release so many of His slaves from the torment of Hell as on the day of Arafa."[29]

Once it was enquired from the Prophet which was the most excellent of acts. He replied, "affirmation

---

[29] Muslim.

of faith in God and His Apostle." He was asked what was next to it, and he said, "Jehad in the way of Allah." On being asked what came after it, the Prophet replied, "Pure and untainted Haj."[30]

Included among the wise and far-reaching regulations governing the Haj pilgrimage is the determination of *Miquats*[31] which fulfils the purpose of imparting a new consciousness to the pilgrim and producing a kind of mental and spiritual awakening in him. He begins to feel that he is approaching an Imperial durbar and has entered its sanctified precincts. But for it, the pilgrims would reach the House of Allah without being psychologically prepared for the event like the uncultured rustics who intrude into the courts of kings and noblemen only to be thrown out unceremoniously.

---

[30] Ibid.

[31] *Miquats* are places marked out on the different sides of the city of Mecca on reaching which a pilgrim coming for the Haj or Umra from a place lying beyond them is required to put on the pilgrim's robe of *Ihrām*.

Commenting on the significance of *Mawaquit*[32] Hazrat Shah Waliullah writes: "The real idea behind the determination of *Mawaquit* is that while, on the one hand, it is enjoined upon the pilgrims to present themselves in Mecca with their hair dishevelled and in a distressed condition, on the other, there is an open difficulty for them in setting forth from their homes with the Ihram wrapped round their bodies-some of whom have to do a month or two of travelling, or even more- some special places have been marked on all sides of Mecca on crossing which it is necessary to put on the Ihram. Care has been taken that these places are well known as points of transit. The *Miquat* for people coming from Medina (i.e., Zul-Hulaifa) is at the farthest distance. It is so because Medina is the centre of Divine Revelation, the citadel of faith, the home of Migration and the first city to embrace Islam at the Call of Allah and the Apostle. The people of Medina, as such, have a greater claim to be in the vanguard of those who strive in the path of Allah and ahead of everyone in worship. As against Jawatha, Taif and Yamama, Medina is counted among the earliest towns to have entered into the fold

[32] Plural of *Miquat*.

of Islam and given proof of single-minded devotion to faith. There is, therefore, no harm if the *Miquat* for it has been fixed so far away."[33]

The pilgrim's robe of Ihram is meant to attune him spiritually to the sublimity of his mission. It brings about in the pilgrim the realisation that he is going on an important errand and presenting himself in the holiest of courts. There is also a complete freedom in it from ostentation. In this way, Ihram occupies the same place in the Haj as *Takbir*[34] does in Salat which takes the worshipper into a new spiritual climate and puts him in as special kind of bondage by taking away his freedom for the time being:

Observations of Hazrat Shah Waliullah:

"Ihram which is worn in the Haj and Umra is like the Takbir of Salat. It is a symbol of believer's faith, sincerity and endeavour. Its purpose is to make the self lowly before God, to make it bow down before Him in

---

[33] *Hujjatullah*, Vol. 11, p. 44

[34] The Formula of *Allah-o-Akbar* recited at the commencement of Namaz.

submission and to serve as an expression of anguish, distress and suffering for His sake."[35]

A definite method has also been prescribed for coming out of the state of Ihram and the discipline that goes with it. It is not that the pilgrim takes off the Ihram all of a sudden and begins to enjoy all the things that were prohibited till then. He does so with a precise formulation of intention (*Niyat*) and in accordance with a definite procedure. Just as a person comes out of the state of Salat by means of *Salam* (Salutation), he divests himself of *Ihram* through *Hulq* (shaving of the hair). As Hazrat Shah Waliullah explains, "The significance of *Hulq* is that by it a method of coming out of the state of Ihram is determined which is not opposed to dignity. If people were left to their own judgement everyone would be acting the way he liked. Besides, it marks the termination of the state of dishevelment that was desired earlier. It is like the turning of the face (*Salam*) in *Salat*."[36]

---

[35] *Hujjatullah*, Vol. II, p. 44.

[36] *Hujjat*, Vol. II, p. 45.

Talbia, again, forms a part of the plan designed to enhance the efficacy of the Haj. The Shariat has stressed its importance, and the holy Prophet also has said that it is preferable to utter it in a loud and full-throated manner. On being asked which Haj was of a higher order, he is reported to have remarked, "The one in which *Talbia* is recited forcefully and the animals are offered in sacrifice properly."[37]

The *Talbia* has an important role to play in stirring up the inner self of the pilgrim, in enkindling the flame of love, devotion and eagerness within him and in arousing in him the desire to beg, beseech and rub his forehead on the ground in the holy precincts of the House of Allah. As the pilgrim utters it, a wave of faith and spirituality surges through his entire existence. It equips him emotionally for the great event and, thus, removes the deficiency from which he is, generally, inclined to suffer owing to pre-occupation with the mundane things of life. When he raises the heart-warming cry of Here, I am O God, Here I am in Thy Presence: Thou art without a partner: All Praise is for

---

[37] Ibn-i-Majah.

Thee, and from Thee are all Blessings! To Thee belongs all Power (and Rule): Thou hast no partner, the inherent meaning and significance of the Haj dawns upon him in its full lustre and solemnity, he is seized with joy and excitement, the cup of love overflows and the flame of Monotheism runs through the depths of his being; he feels restless and a genuine mental and spiritual affinity between him and Hazrat Ibrahim and the sacred Prophet and his Companions and the bearers of his message is created and he becomes one with them.

Sanctity of Time and Space

God has bestowed two special 'sanctities' upon the Haj, the sanctity of time and the sanctity of space, due to which the pilgrim remains alive to the grandeur of the occasion and the solemnity of his own responsibility. He is zealously vigilant in his conduct and never becomes neglectful of the unique spiritual atmosphere surrounding the Pilgrimage.

﴿إِنَّ عِدَّةَ ٱلشُّهُورِ عِندَ ٱللَّهِ ٱثْنَا عَشَرَ شَهْرًا فِي كِتَٰبِ ٱللَّهِ يَوْمَ خَلَقَ ٱلسَّمَٰوَٰتِ وَٱلْأَرْضَ مِنْهَآ أَرْبَعَةٌ حُرُمٌ ۚ ذَٰلِكَ ٱلدِّينُ ٱلْقَيِّمُ ۚ فَلَا تَظْلِمُوا۟ فِيهِنَّ أَنفُسَكُمْ ۚ﴾

Indeed, the number of months ordained by Allah is twelve—in Allah's Record[1] since the day He created the heavens and the earth—of which four are sacred. That is the Right Way. So do not wrong one another during these months. (9: 36)

And also:

﴿يَسْـَٔلُونَكَ عَنِ ٱلشَّهْرِ ٱلْحَرَامِ قِتَالٍ فِيهِ ۖ قُلْ قِتَالٌ فِيهِ كَبِيرٌ ۖ﴾

They ask you ⌜O Prophet⌝ about fighting in the sacred months. Say, "Fighting during these months is a great sin. (2: 217)

It is related that the Prophet once said, "Verily, Time has returned to its original state-as it was on the day on which God created the heavens and the earth.

Four months are sacred in it: Zi-Quad, Zil-Hijja, Muharrum and Rajab."[38]

As for the sanctity of space, we read the following in the Quran:

﴿إِنَّمَآ أُمِرْتُ أَنْ أَعْبُدَ رَبَّ هَٰذِهِ ٱلْبَلْدَةِ ٱلَّذِى حَرَّمَهَا وَلَهُۥ كُلُّ شَىْءٍ ۖ وَأُمِرْتُ أَنْ أَكُونَ مِنَ ٱلْمُسْلِمِينَ ﴿٩١﴾﴾

Say, ⌜O Prophet⌝, "I have only been commanded to worship the Lord of this city ⌜of Mecca⌝, Who has made it sacred, and to Him belongs everything. And I am commanded to be one of those who ⌜fully⌝ submit ⌜to Him⌝. (27: 91)

It is related by Ibn-i-Abbas that the Prophet said on the occasion of the victory of Mecca, "Migration has ceased from today but Jehad and Niyat remain. Start out at once when you are called up for faith." He also remarked, "God has granted sanctity to this town from the day on which He created the heavens and the earth. This sacredness will endure till the end of the world. Even before me warfare was prohibited in it and to me

---

[38] Muslim.

also it has been allowed only for a short time of the day. Now it is forbidden, with the sanctity of Allah, till the Last Day. In it, neither a thorn can be plucked, nor a straw broken, nor a bird or animal driven for game nor an article dropped (by any one) picked up. "Upon it, Abbas enquired, "O Prophet of God! Can *Ikhir*[39] also not be pulled out (which was often needed by the people)?" The Prophet replied, "Of course, with the exception of *Ikhir*."

To commit a sin within the bounds of Haram[40] is, in any case, a grievous matter. But, according to some doctors, even the intention to commit a sin in it is an offence and, in their support, they cite the following verse of the Quran:

﴿وَمَن يُرِدْ فِيهِ بِإِلْحَادٍ بِظُلْمٍ نُّذِقْهُ مِنْ عَذَابٍ أَلِيمٍ ﴿٢٥﴾﴾

Along with whoever intends to deviate by doing wrong in it,[2] We will cause them to taste a painful punishment. (22: 25)

---

[39] A kind of aromatic grass.

[40] The city of Mecca along with a certain outlying territory on all sides is called Haram.

Ibn-i-Katheer, for instance, asserts that "the distinction of the Haram is that here even a person who thinks of committing a sin is liable to be called to account and punished no matter whether he carries it into action or not with the sanctity of time and space, a number of special regulations have been prescribed for the sanctity of Ihram as well. Hunting, for example, is forbidden to one who is in the state of wearing it. Says the Quran:

﴿يَٰٓأَيُّهَا ٱلَّذِينَ ءَامَنُواْ لَا تَقْتُلُواْ ٱلصَّيْدَ وَأَنتُمْ حُرُمٌۚ﴾

O believers! Do not kill game while on pilgrimage. (5: 95)

﴿أُحِلَّ لَكُمْ صَيْدُ ٱلْبَحْرِ وَطَعَامُهُۥ مَتَٰعًا لَّكُمْ وَلِلسَّيَّارَةِۖ وَحُرِّمَ عَلَيْكُمْ صَيْدُ ٱلْبَرِّ مَا دُمْتُمْ حُرُمًاۗ وَٱتَّقُواْ ٱللَّهَ ٱلَّذِىٓ إِلَيْهِ تُحْشَرُونَ ٩٦﴾

It is lawful for you to hunt and eat seafood, as a provision for you and for travellers. But hunting on land is forbidden to you while on pilgrimage. Be mindful of Allah to Whom you all will be gathered. (5: 96)

To quote from Hazrat Shah Waliullah's *Hujjatullah- ul-Baligha* "These things are forbidden to the pilgrim who is wearing the Ihram so that he attained the state of humbleness, renouncement of ostentation, and dishevelment, and unkemptness, the reverent fear of God and of His punishment became dominant in him and he was not caught in the web of (worldly) desires and interests. Hunting has been included among the prohibited things because it also falls within the sphere of self-indulgence and is a kind of entertainment."[41]

For many a pilgrim the journey of the Haj is a long one, taking a lot of time.

And proclaim unto mankind the Pilgrimage.

﴿وَأَذِّن فِي ٱلنَّاسِ بِٱلۡحَجِّ يَأۡتُوكَ رِجَالٗا وَعَلَىٰ كُلِّ ضَامِرٖ يَأۡتِينَ
مِن كُلِّ فَجٍّ عَمِيقٖ ٢٧﴾

Call ⌜all⌝ people to the pilgrimage. They will come to you on foot and on every lean camel from every distant path. (22: 27)

---

[41] Vol. II, p. 44.

During the journey, the pilgrim passes through various experiences. He comes into contact with different people and has to live among strangers for days and weeks. In its situations can arise that test his patience and make him irritable. He can be provoked to be quarrelsome or incited to commit other misdeeds. Often, he is inclined to be petty and mean and to behave in a manner he considered disgraceful even at home. Sometimes, he is guilty of a moral indiscretion which is plainly injurious to the spirit of his mission. All such things have been particularly forbidden to the pilgrim since there was a greater likelihood of their occurrence during the Haj.

﴿ٱلْحَجُّ أَشْهُرٌ مَّعْلُومَٰتٌ ۚ فَمَن فَرَضَ فِيهِنَّ ٱلْحَجَّ فَلَا رَفَثَ
وَلَا فُسُوقَ وَلَا جِدَالَ فِى ٱلْحَجِّ ۗ وَمَا تَفْعَلُوا۟ مِنْ خَيْرٍ يَعْلَمْهُ
ٱللَّهُ ۗ وَتَزَوَّدُوا۟ فَإِنَّ خَيْرَ ٱلزَّادِ ٱلتَّقْوَىٰ ۚ وَٱتَّقُونِ يَٰٓأُو۟لِى
ٱلْأَلْبَٰبِ ١٩٧﴾

⌜Commitment to⌝ pilgrimage is made in appointed months. Whoever commits to ⌜performing⌝ pilgrimage, let them stay away from intimate relations, foul language, and arguments during pilgrimage. Whatever good you do, Allah ⌜fully⌝ knows of it. Take ⌜necessary⌝ provisions ⌜for the journey⌝—surely the best provision is righteousness. And be mindful of Me, O people of reason! (2: 197)

These teachings and regulations (related as they are directly to mind and conscience, deed and intent, and time and space) have vested the Haj with a sense of solemnity and self-denial which is wholly its own. The uplifting influences the rites of the Haj exert on life and the inclination for self-searching and moral and spiritual restraint and correction they produce in the pilgrim is not equalled by a similar event or observance in any other community. This uniqueness goes to confirm the truth of the celestial Tradition of the Prophet which says: "He who performs the Haj and commits no lustful act during it and does not disobey God, (in any other way), will return from it as pure and sinless as he was at the time of his birth."

Farewell Haj

The holy Prophet had not performed the Haj since his migration to Medina. He set out for Mecca with the intention of performing the Haj in the month of Zil-Hijja in the tenth year of Migration. The whole of Arabia was stirred as the news spread and about a lakh[42] of Muslims thronged to Mecca to join him on the Pilgrimage. This pilgrimage is popularly known as the Farewell Haj for it was not only the first but also the last Haj performed by the sacred Prophet and in it he bade farewell to his followers and imparted to them his last advice and testament.

The Farewell Haj is worthy of being remembered as a portent of Allah and a miracle of the holy Prophet. It is unique in many ways and commands a distinctive place among the acts of religious devotion performed by the Divine Apostles. It is also of unequalled significance in the sense that a vast body of men were afforded the opportunity of associating themselves with the Prophet, of emulating his example, carrying out his instructions, observing his movements and recording the minutest details of his daily life. From one generation to another, the Ummat has striven hard to obtain guidance from it

---

[42] Meaning a hundred thousand.

and to evolve rules on the basis of every single item of what the Prophet said or did during the blessed journey.

The Muslims have spared themselves nothing by way of time and industry in the compilation and preservation of the record of this Pilgrimage. They have brought to bear a rare power of observation and sense of under- standing and responsibility to this task. But it has not merely been an intellectual accomplishment for we have enough experience of how important details are left out of biographies and travel-accounts of great men. It is, in fact, a marvel of love, of the tender emotion, which is always, alive, alert and watchful and to which even a particle of dust bearing an association with the beloved is more precious than gold.

Throughout the long and hallowed journey love remained a close companion of intellect. From the time the Prophet announced his decision to go on Pilgrimage till his return to Medina this fellowship was not broken for a moment. The two kept a close watch on all his sayings and doings and have left behind for the Ummat and the succeeding generations a record so complete and accurate that from it a Muslim can know clearly about everything that took place during the whole course of the Pilgrimage-how did the Prophet travel from Medina to Mecca, what happened during his visits to Mina and Arafat, and on his way back to Mecca, and, finally, on his return journey to Medina. In the mirror of it he can see the Prophet talking, preaching and exhorting, doing the *Sa'ee*, performing the Tawaf and completing the other rites. Thanks to it, he can participate, intellectually and spiritually, in all these events and incidents. As a Muslim reads the account of the Farewell Haj the invisible becomes the visible for him and the past, the present.

From all pointers and attending circumstances this Haj of the Prophet was destined to take place the way it did. It was not a chance occurrence but had come to pass designedly and at the most appropriate time. That it materialised so late was not without significance. It was when Islam had spread throughout the Peninsula of Arabia, the number of Muslims had swelled, faith had grown in strength and love had mellowed, the minds and hearts of men had become receptive and they were willing to learn and imbibe new knowledge, the hour of the Prophet's departure from the world was drawing near and it seemed necessary that he bade farewell to his followers. It was in these circumstances that the holy Prophet undertook the Pilgrimage so that he could meet the Muslims and inform them, for the last time, about the modes and formalities of worship, fulfil his mission as a witness of Allah and take from them the pledge of adherence to the Divine path and the way of the Islamic Shariat after he had passed away, and demolish the last vestiges of idolatry and paganism. The Farewell Haj was, indeed, the equivalent to a thousand sermons and exhortations.

It would be a sheer waste of time to try to find a parallel of the wonderful manner in which the minutest details of the happenings in the entire course of the Farewell Pilgrimage of the Prophet have been preserved in the descriptions of the journeys undertaken by other men of eminence, both temporal and spiritual. The record made available by most of the communities of their Apostles is defective and incomplete. What we know, for example, about the life of Jesus does not, according to Encyclopaedia Britannica, cover more than fifty days of his career on earth.[43]

---

[43] Vol. XIII., pp. 16-17.

Since the Haj is performed only once in a year and in view of the promise of an immense reward and forgiveness it carries and the extraordinary preparations that are made for it and hardships borne and the exceptional restrictions that are placed on the pilgrims and the unusual rites that are to be carried out, it is essential that one should do one's utmost to learn and perform the Haj in the best of manner by following the example of the sacred Prophet and conducting oneself in accordance with the standard set by him. In this lies the primary importance of the Farewell Haj and it will continue to serve as the criterion of perfection for Muslims for all time to come.

Pilgrimage in Other Religions

There is no religious group or community which may not have its holy shrines and places of pilgrimage. In every faith there are some sacred places to which its followers travel at a certain time and as an act of religious devotion. This is so because it fulfils a great human need and satisfies a basic spiritual urge. Man, as we have said already, is always in the quest of an object through which he can gratify his inborn feelings of love and fidelity. He needs a profound event, a prolonged ceremony through which he can make amends for his serious transgressions and obtain release from the stinging reflections of his conscience and the reproach of society. Within him there is a persistent desire for an impressive congregation which may be solely inspired by religious and spiritual motives and free from all other considerations. When we look at history, we find that no nation or society has ever been without its shrines and places hallowed by memory where people have got together for offering up oblations and making entreaties to the Almighty (or gods and goddesses of their own creation). In the words of the Quran:

﴿وَلِكُلِّ أُمَّةٍ جَعَلْنَا مَنسَكًا لِّيَذْكُرُوا ٱسْمَ ٱللَّهِ عَلَىٰ مَا رَزَقَهُم مِّنۢ بَهِيمَةِ ٱلْأَنْعَٰمِ ۗ فَإِلَٰهُكُمْ إِلَٰهٌ وَٰحِدٌ فَلَهُۥٓ أَسْلِمُوا ۗ وَبَشِّرِ ٱلْمُخْبِتِينَ ٣٤﴾

For every community We appointed a rite of sacrifice so that they may pronounce the Name of Allah over the sacrificial animals He has provided for them. For your God is only One God, so submit yourselves to Him ⌜alone⌝. And give good news ⌜O Prophet⌝ to the humble. (22: 34)

﴿لِّكُلِّ أُمَّةٍ جَعَلْنَا مَنسَكًا هُمْ نَاسِكُوهُ ۖ فَلَا يُنَازِعُنَّكَ فِي ٱلْأَمْرِ ۚ وَٱدْعُ إِلَىٰ رَبِّكَ ۖ إِنَّكَ لَعَلَىٰ هُدًى مُّسْتَقِيمٍ ﴿٦٧﴾﴾

For every community We appointed a code of life to follow. So do not let them dispute with you ⌜O Prophet⌝ in this matter. And invite ⌜all⌝ to your Lord, for you are truly on the Right Guidance. (22: 67)

Excavators and archaeologists have unearthed incontrovertible evidence in support of this contention. History also tells that the institution of pilgrimage has always been present among the various peoples and communities of the world. But it is very difficult to get to the bottom of these rites and obtain an adequate knowledge of the rules and ceremonies governing them. What we have so far been able to learn is only of a fragmentary and speculative nature on the basis of which no precise picture can be drawn.

The Jewish and Christian faiths are nearest to us in the matter of the pilgrimage. Both of these have seen long stretches of history and enlightenment, and chroniclers, too, have done full justice to them. Even now their adherents make two of the most advanced peoples of the world, culturally, educationally and politically. Ancient monuments and other sacred places in Jerusalem are still the objects of veneration and they have been making a pilgrimage to that eternal city from the days of old. But when we compare it with the Islamic Haj the image of the Jewish or Christian pilgrimage that emerges in the mind is, at least, weak and hazy.

We will now reproduce a summary of what appears about the pilgrimage in Judaism in the tenth volume of the *Jewish Encyclopaedia.*[44]

The pilgrimage to Jerusalem, which was called *Re'iyah* (meaning the appearance) used to take place on one of the three festivals of Passover, Shabn'ot and Sukkot. The Mishnah says that all were under obligation to appear, except minors, women, the blind, the aged and the sick. A minor, in this case, was defined as one who was too young to be taken by his father to Jerusalem. According to the Mosaic Law, everyone was to take an offering, through the value of it was not fixed. While the appearance of women and infant males was

---

[44] pp. 35-37.

not obligatory, they usually accompanied their husbands and fathers in all public gatherings.

Gesius Florus, who lived in Jerusalem from 64 to 66 A.D., counted that 256,500 lambs were sacrificed at the one Passover Festival, and allowing ten persons to one lamb this would make 2,565,000 pilgrims. The Tosefta records that on one occasion 1,200,000 lambs were offered in sacrifice which would make a total of 12,000,000 pilgrims. These figures are evidently exaggerated.

The pilgrimage to Jerusalem did not cease with the destruction of the temple. The Turkish conquest under Salahuddin (1187) secured to the Oriental Jews the privilege of visiting Jerusalem and the sacred places. Among the Eastern Jews, especially those of Babylonia and Kurdistan, it has been the custom from the 14th Century onward to go on pilgrimage at least once a year, many of them actually walking the whole distance. The era of the Crusades evidently encouraged pilgrimage of Jews from Europe.

The expulsion of the Jews from Spain in 1492 and the consequent settlement of many exiles in Turkish territory largely increased the number of pilgrims. The goal of their journeys was chiefly the tomb of Samuel the Prophet at Ramah where they held annual communions and celebrations.

The Jews of Palestine complain of the lack of interest on the part of their co-religionists elsewhere as compared with the thousands of Christians who avail themselves of modern opportunities to visit the Holy Land.

Pilgrimages are made usually on fixed days in the year, called by the Oriental and North African Jews as 'days of Zi'arah. On such days it is customary to visit the tombs or relics of certain personages who in early or medieval times were famous as kings or Prophets for their holy lives. The days of pilgrimage are celebrated by prayers, rejoicings and popular festivals.

In Jerusalem a crowd of Jews gathers before the western wall of the Temple of Solomon every Friday evening and on the eves of the feast days as well as on 23 successive days from the eve of the 17th of Tammuz to the 9th of Ab. On the latter date the religious service occurs at midnight.

As for the institution of pilgrimage among the Christians an outline of it is reproduced below from the 10th volume of the *Encyclopaedia of Religion and Ethics.*[45]

"As pilgrimage", says it is a journey undertaken to visit sacred places, such as, the scenes of our Lord's earthly life in Palestine, the 'threshold of the Apostles' at Rome or the shrines of saints and martyrs.

"It was natural for a Christian to wish to tread again the paths treaden by the Saviour, though the first generations of Christians did not seem to feel as strongly as their successors. From the 3rd Century certainly, the sacred places were visited. Many Christians have felt far greater attraction to the scene of their Lord's passion and resurrection than to those of His earthly ministry.

"From the 13th Century pilgrimages to the Holy land, though still frequent, were less numerous than those to Rome. Next after Jerusalem, Rome was the city which drew the largest number of pilgrims. The causes which contributed to the rise of the Papacy made Rome a pilgrim resort; more specially the tombs of St. Peter

---

[45] p. 18.

and St. Paul exalted it into the goal whither Roman Catholics flocked.

"One centre of interest was the catacombs. A first used as burial places, they afterwards became sacred places, hallowed by the bones of martyrs and visited by thousands of pilgrims. The pilgrims have never ceased to visit Rome; the large number of Churches have been continuous sources of attraction."

This was only about a few places of pilgrimage. There is a bewildering abundance of relics, tombs and shrines not only in Palestine but in all the countries inhabited by Jews and Christians. A detailed account of the graves of saints and martyrs and other sacred places is given in the two monumental works we have referred to above. In them the contributors have, further, mentioned the days on which the pilgrimage was to be made and the different rituals that were considered necessary on such occasions.

When one looks at the excessive attachment of the Jewish and Christian peoples (the 'People of the Book') to shrines and the exaggerated religious fervour with which they undertook long and tedious journeys to them and which had, ultimately, pushed them into the lap of Polytheism it becomes apparent why the holy Prophet had taken such great pains to put an end to the custom. He was apprehensive of the unholy practices becoming rampant among the torch-bearers of Monotheism and the last of the Divinely ordained communities with which rested the responsibility of lending guidance to mankind till the day of the Last Judgement. He ordered his own grave to be kept free from all Polytheistic ways and performances. It was his chief anxiety during his last illness.

It is related by Hazrat Ayesha and Abdullah-bin-Abbas that "when the Prophet fell ill, he would cover his venerable face with the sheet and when he became restless, he would cast the sheet away. In this condition he said, "The curse of God be upon the Jews and Christians who have converted the graves of their Prophets into places of performing the prostration. He was, in this way, warning his followers against such customs and practices."[46]

---

[46] Bukhari.

It is, further, related by Hazrat Abu Huraira that the sacred Prophet once said, "May God destroy the Jews. They have made the graves of their Prophets into places of worship."[47]

It is related by Hazrat Ayesha that once Umm-i-Salma was talking to the Prophet about the Synagogue of Maria she had visited in Abyssinia. She spoke of the paintings she had seen in it. The Prophet, thereupon, remarked, "These are the people who, when a good or pious person died among them, used to build a temple on his grave. They are the worst of the creatures of Allah.[48]

Yet another Tradition reads: "O Allah: Let my grave not be an idol to which worship may be offered. Allah is severely displeased with those who have made the graves of their Prophets into places of worship."[49]

The Prophet has forbidden his followers to make a journey specifically with the object of visiting a tomb or shrine. He said, "A journey, with intention and

---

[47] Ibid

[48] Ibid

[49] Ibid

preparation, is permissible only to three mosques *Masjid Haram*[50], *Masjid-un-Nabi*[51] and *Masjid-i-Aqsa*[52]."

He has, thus, made the Muslim Millet safe against the perverting influence of tombs and shrines which had led many a community into Polytheism and idolatry.

Unfortunately, however, some sections of Muslims failed to abide by the Prophet's advice and went astray although it was what had kept him worried even on the death-bed. They, too, succumbed to the spell of tombs and shrines and began to visit them out of religious devotion covering long distances and undergoing all sorts of difficulties. They took to prostrating themselves before the graves of holy men and making their vows and petitions to them and showing reverential respect in many other ways, as was the habit of the Jews and Christians.

The prophecy of the sacred Prophet has been fulfilled to the very letter that "you will go wholly in the same direction as the earlier peoples did. If they will

---

[50] At Mecca

[51] At Madina

[52] At Jerusalem

move by a span you, too, will move by a span, and if they will move by a cubit you, too, will move by a cubit."[53]

The tombs and shrines (many of which were false and fictitious) not only encroached upon the right of the mosques but, sometimes, also took the place of Masjid-i-Haram and the House of Ka'aba. The ignorant and the unknowing began to gather around them in large numbers and soon it gave rise to the practice of celebrating the *Urs*[54] and holding fairs in commemoration of the death of the holy men with whom these were associated. The condition of these people has been eloquently depicted by Ibn-i-Taimiyah in these words, "The tombs among them are crammed

---

[53] It is related by Abu Sa'eed Khudri that the Prophet once said: 'You will follow the example of the preceding communities span by span and cubit by cubit so much so that if they will crawl into the hole of a lizard, you too will do the same." The Prophet was asked whether by the preceding communities he meant the Jews and Christians. "Who else?" he replied.

[54] An annual festival held at the tombs of religious divines to commemorate their death.

with people while the mosques are empty and deserted."[55]

A traveller going round the Muslim World will witness, from place to place, the depressing spectacle of Polytheistic practices being performed at tombs, shrines and *Imambaras* (to which large properties are endowed) and dialogues carried on with the religious divines buried in them in a manner most revolting to the spirit of Islam.

Among the religions of India, namely, Hinduism, Buddhism and Jainism, there is a profusion of temples and other places of pilgrimage that are held sacred owing to their association with some special incident like the receiving of enlightenment by a saint or holy man or the appearance (according to the belief of their adherents) of a god or goddess in a manner outside of nature. The number of religious fairs and bathing festivals in these communities is very large.

The places of pilgrimage are mostly situated on the banks of River Ganges where tens and thousands of

---

[55] *Minhaj-us-Sunnah*, Vol. I, pp. 130-131.

persons collect for a dip in its holy waters. Some of the bathing festivals are held once or twice a year and others once in two years. There are also bathing festivals and fairs whose turn comes after many years like the Kumbh Mela at Prayag which is held every twelfth year and attracts millions of pilgrims from all parts of the country. The rituals also vary from place to place reflecting the conceptual differences of the sects that go to make these communities.

These fairs are tied to mythological lore and legends relating to deeds and relationships of the deities. On seeing them one is amazed at the miracle of the Quran which, at the time of the construction of the House of Ka'aba, took care, first of all, to deal a deathly blow to Polytheism, mythical lore and fairyism in which the rites and ceremonies of Pilgrimage in other communities have got steeped. It says:

﴿ذَٰلِكَۖ وَمَن يُعَظِّمۡ حُرُمَٰتِ ٱللَّهِ فَهُوَ خَيۡرٞ لَّهُۥ عِندَ رَبِّهِۦۗ
وَأُحِلَّتۡ لَكُمُ ٱلۡأَنۡعَٰمُ إِلَّا مَا يُتۡلَىٰ عَلَيۡكُمۡۖ فَٱجۡتَنِبُواْ
ٱلرِّجۡسَ مِنَ ٱلۡأَوۡثَٰنِ وَٱجۡتَنِبُواْ قَوۡلَ ٱلزُّورِ ٣٠ حُنَفَآءَ لِلَّهِ غَيۡرَ

مُشْرِكِينَ بِهِۦۚ وَمَن يُشْرِكْ بِٱللَّهِ فَكَأَنَّمَا خَرَّ مِنَ ٱلسَّمَآءِ
فَتَخْطَفُهُ ٱلطَّيْرُ أَوْ تَهْوِى بِهِ ٱلرِّيحُ فِى مَكَانٍ سَحِيقٍ ﴿٣١﴾

That is so. And whoever honours the rituals of Allah, it is best for them in the sight of their Lord. The ⌜meat of⌝ cattle has been made lawful for you, except what has ⌜already⌝ been recited to you. So, shun the impurity of idolatry and shun words of falsehood. Be upright ⌜in devotion⌝ to Allah, associating none with Him ⌜in worship⌝. (22: 30-31)

This was a description in passing, of the form and formalities of Pilgrimage in some of the leading religions of the world whose adherents run into millions.

Remarks Hazrat Shah Waliullah: "The foundation of Pilgrimage is present in all communities. A place which might be sacred in their eyes as a landmark of God or on account of its association with the deeds, sacrifices and penances of their precursors was needed by all of them so that it could be helpful in reviving the memory of the favourites of the Lord and their achievements. The House of Allah enjoys a preference over such places because clear signs of Allah can be seen there, and it was built by Hazrat Ibrahim who is the spiritual progenitor of most of the nations. He built the First House at a barren and désérted place at the command of Allah for his worship and the Haj Pilgrimage. If, aside of it, anything exists at any place it has definitely got polluted with Polytheism, perversion and innovation."[56]

It is impossible to disagree with what Hazrat Shah Waliullah has said. The following verse of the Quran will come automatically to the mind of anyone who compares the Islamic Haj with the Pilgrimage in other faiths.

﴿لِّكُلِّ أُمَّةٍ جَعَلْنَا مَنسَكًا هُمْ نَاسِكُوهُ ۖ فَلَا يُنَازِعُنَّكَ فِي
ٱلْأَمْرِ ۚ وَٱدْعُ إِلَىٰ رَبِّكَ ۖ إِنَّكَ لَعَلَىٰ هُدًى مُّسْتَقِيمٍ ٦٧﴾

For every community We appointed a code of life to follow. So do not let them dispute with you ⌜O Prophet⌝ in this matter. And invite ⌜all⌝ to your Lord, for you are truly on the Right Guidance. (22: 67)

---

[56] *Hujjat*, Vol. I, p. 59

Reformative Role of Islam

Islam has also played a reformative role of profound significance in the sphere of Pilgrimage. The Pagans had introduced numerous perverse innovations and rituals in the Haj destroying its spirit and doing a tremendous harm to its aims and advantages. Paganish pride, tribal vanity and the discriminatory behaviour of the Quraish were mainly responsible for it. The holy Quran and the Shariat put an end to the lamentable state of affairs by doing away with each and every vestige of the days of Ignorance and giving to mankind something the like of which it had never seen before.

During the pre-Islamic days, the Quraish did not go to Arafat with other pilgrims but stayed back at Haram. They said that they belonged to the family of God and were the custodians of the House of Ka'aba. They, thus, sought to assert the superiority of their position and to perpetuate their privileges. Their Paganish pride and tribal arrogance was brought to an end by God and it was enjoined upon them to do as the others did and make the halt at Arafat.

﴿ثُمَّ أَفِيضُوا۟ مِنْ حَيْثُ أَفَاضَ ٱلنَّاسُ وَٱسْتَغْفِرُوا۟ ٱللَّهَ ۚ إِنَّ ٱللَّهَ غَفُورٌ رَّحِيمٌ ١٩٩﴾

Then go forth with the rest of the pilgrims. And seek Allah's forgiveness. Surely Allah is All-Forgiving, Most Merciful. (2: 199)

Hazrat Ayesha relates that the Quraish and those who followed their example halted at Muzdalifa, and they were known as Hums, while the rest of the pilgrims stopped at Arafat. But when Islam came, God commanded His Apostle to proceed to Arafat and make a halt there also, and then, return with the other pilgrims. This is what is implied in the Quranic verse: Then hasten onward from the place whence the multitude hasteneth onward. Ibn-i-Kathir says that Ibn-i-Abbas, Mujahid, Ata, Qatada, Suddi and other theological doctors also are of the same view. Ibn-i-Jareer, too, has related in the same manner and there is a general agreement over it in the Ummat.

Like the fairs of Okaz, Zul Majanna and Zul Majaz, the Haj, too, had become an occasion for flourish, pomposity, competition and polemics. It was the habit of the Pagans to be on the lookout for opportunities of self-glorification. They made use of every festival and congregation to show themselves off in high feather and to talk about their ancestors in a vainglorious manner. The congregation of Mina was ideally suited for the display of their crude tribal instincts and, hence, it was forbidden by Allah and a better alternative was provided to them.

﴿فَإِذَا قَضَيْتُم مَّنَٰسِكَكُمْ فَٱذْكُرُوا۟ ٱللَّهَ كَذِكْرِكُمْ
ءَابَآءَكُمْ أَوْ أَشَدَّ ذِكْرًا﴾

When you have fulfilled your sacred rites, praise Allah as you used to praise your forefathers ⌜before Islam⌝, or even more passionately. (2: 200)

It is related by Hazrat Ibn-i Abbas that "the Pagan Arabs used to compete with each other in vulgar ostentation and self-praise during the season of the Haj. They bragged about the chivalry, nobility and hospitality of their ancestors, and related how they fed others, carried their loads and shed rivers of blood for their sake. They had no other occupation than to praise their forefathers. It was at such a time that the Quranic verse was revealed: Remember Allah as ye remember you ancestors or with a more lively remembrance."

With the passage of time the Haj had lost much of its purity, simplicity and sanctity and become just another fair in which all sorts of games and shows were held and brawls and altercations took place. It all was condemned by God who proclaimed:

﴿فَمَن فَرَضَ فِيهِنَّ ٱلْحَجَّ فَلَا رَفَثَ وَلَا فُسُوقَ وَلَا جِدَالَ فِي ٱلْحَجِّ﴾

Whoever commits to ⌜performing⌝ pilgrimage, let them stay away from intimate relations, foul language, and arguments during pilgrimage. (2: 197)

Ibn-i-Kathir tells that it was related by Abdullah bin Wahab, on the authority of Maalik, that "the occasion for the revelation of the Divine Commandment, Let there be no angry conversation on the Pilgrimage was that the Quraish used to stay at Muzdalifa near *Mash'ar-i-Haram* and they wrangled among themselves. A group of them would say that it was in the right and the other would say that it was in the right. This was the position so far as I know; but God knows best."

Likewise, when the Pagan Arabs killed the animals as a sacrifice to their god, they placed their flesh before them and sprinkled their blood on them. Upon it, the following verse of the Quran was revealed:

﴿لَن يَنَالَ ٱللَّهَ لُحُومُهَا﴾

Neither their meat nor blood reaches Allah. (22: 37)

It is related by Ibn-i-Kathir that "the Pagans used to throw the flesh and blood of the sacrificed animals at the House of Ka'aba. On seeing it, the holy Companions side to the Prophet that they were more deserving of the gift. At this, the following verse was revealed: Their flesh reaches not Allah, nor their blood, but the devotion from you reacheth Him."

Another custom among the Pagan Arabs was that when they did the Niyat for the Haj, they refrained from going into their houses through the doors as it was considered sinful. As long as they remained in the state of *Ihram*, they entered into them by scaling the walls.

This, too, was prohibited by the Quran which said that there was no virtue in it.

﴿وَلَيْسَ ٱلْبِرُّ بِأَن تَأْتُوا۟ ٱلْبُيُوتَ مِن ظُهُورِهَا وَلَٰكِنَّ ٱلْبِرَّ مَنِ ٱتَّقَىٰ ۗ﴾

Righteousness is not in entering your houses from the back doors. Rather, righteousness is to be mindful ⌜of Allah⌝. (2: 189)

Some people avoided taking the wherewithal of the journey with them when they set out on the Haj pilgrimage. They thought that it was against the spirit of reliance upon God to take provisions with them. "We are the guests of God", they said, "Why should we take upon ourselves to make arrangements for our meals and other wants?" Yet they felt no disgrace in begging for their requirements on the way. It was supposed to be an act of penance and resignation. This practice, also, was forbidden by God.

﴿وَتَزَوَّدُوا۟ فَإِنَّ خَيْرَ ٱلزَّادِ ٱلتَّقْوَىٰ ۚ﴾

Take ⌜necessary⌝ provisions ⌜for the journey⌝—surely the best provision is righteousness. (2: 197)

It is related by Ibn-i-Khathir that some people started on the journey in such a condition that they carried no provisions with them and were empty-handed. They would say: 'We are going on pilgrimage to the House of God. Will He not feed us?" It was to discourage them that the verse, So, make provision......, was reveal- ed denoting that the pilgrims should take enough provisions to meet their needs and save them from stretching a begging hand before others.

Again, the Pagans considered it sinful to engage in trade during the season of the Haj, and, thus, a lawful activity was rendered unlawful by them. It is related in Bukhari from Ibn-i-Abbas that in the days of Ignorance the markets of 'Okaz, Zul Majanna and Zull Majaz were famous, but trade was forbidden during the season of the Pilgrimage. Upon it, the following verse was revealed:

﴿لَيْسَ عَلَيْكُمْ جُنَاحٌ أَن تَبْتَغُوا۟ فَضْلًا مِّن رَّبِّكُمْ﴾

There is no blame on you for seeking the bounty of your Lord ⌜during this journey⌝. (2: 198)

A most abominable custom was that some people performed the circumambulation of the House of Ka'aba naked saying that they could not carry out the ritual dressed in clothes in which they committed sins. The Paganish practice was a standing invitation to lewdness and perversion. Upon it, the following verse was revealed.

﴿يَٰبَنِيٓ ءَادَمَ خُذُواْ زِينَتَكُمۡ عِندَ كُلِّ مَسۡجِدٖ﴾

O Children of Adam! Dress properly whenever you are at worship. (7: 31)

Awfi relates on the authority of Ibn-i-Abbas that "some people did the circumambulation round the House of Ka'aba in nude. To them God sent down the command of Zeenat (meaning adornment) which signifies a dress that covers the parts of the body that are to be covered and is also seemly and respectable. Ibn-i-Kathir writes that Mujahid, Ata, Ibrahim Nakh'ee, Saeed bin Jubair, Qatada, Suddi, Zahak, Maalik and Zohri have taken the same view of this verse, and they all are agreed that it was revealed in respect of the Polytheists who used to circumambulate round the House of Ka'aba without wearing any clothes.

In Bukhari it is related from Ibn-i-Abbas that "the holy Prophet had directed the delegation he sent under the leadership of Hazrat Abu Bakr a year before the Farewell Haj to proclaim on the sacrificial day that after that year no Polytheist was to perform the Haj, nor could anyone carry out the circumambulation of the House of Ka'aba naked."

Some of the Pagan Arabs believed that the ritual of walking between the hills of Safa and Marwa should not be observed. The following verse was revealed in that connection.

﴿إِنَّ ٱلصَّفَا وَٱلْمَرْوَةَ مِن شَعَآئِرِ ٱللَّهِ ۖ فَمَنْ حَجَّ ٱلْبَيْتَ أَوِ ٱعْتَمَرَ فَلَا جُنَاحَ عَلَيْهِ أَن يَطَّوَّفَ بِهِمَا ۚ﴾

Indeed, ⌜the hills of⌝ Ṣafa and Marwah are among the symbols of Allah. So, whoever makes the major or minor pilgrimage to the ⌜Sacred⌝ House, let them walk between ⌜the two hills⌝. (2: 158)

It is related by Orwah that once Hazrat Ayesha enquired from him what was meant by the verse, Lo! the mountains of As-Safa and Al-Marwa are the Landmarks of Allah......... He replied that it meant that there was no sin in going around the hills of Safa and Marwa. She, thereupon, remarked, "My nephew! You are wrong. Had it meant what you say it would have read: It is no sin for him who does not go around them. The verse was revealed in these circumstances that the Ansars, before the dawn of Islam, used to pay reverential homage to the idol of Manat which was installed near Musallah and he who did so regarded the Tawaf of Safa and Marwa to be sinful. Later they enquired about it from the Prophet and said that during the days of Ignorance they regarded as incorrect the Tawaf of Safa and Marwa. Upon it the verse (quoted above) was revealed." Hazrat Ayesha went on to say that the Prophet then instituted the practice of the Tawaf (of Safa and Marwa) which now no one can abrogate. It is related on the authority of Mohammad bin Yusuf in Bukhari that "I enquired about Safa and Marwa from Anas and he replied that 'earlier we considered it (the Tawaf of the two hills) to be a sign of Paganism and on the advent of Islam we abandoned it. Thereupon, the verse was revealed."

The Islamic Shariat, through these far-reaching changes, restored the magnificent institution of the Haj to its pristine glory and now it has been protected and made safe against every kind of pollution and distortion.

www.ingramcontent.com/pod-product-compliance
Ingram Content Group UK Ltd.
Pitfield, Milton Keynes, MK11 3LW, UK
UKHW021359190726
13845UKWH00028B/771

9 789394 770638